Praise for
Spoke by Spoke: How a Broken Back and a Broken Bike Led to a Wholehearted Life

Most people write from their knowledge. Some people write from their experience. And then there are those who are blessed to write from both. Terry is certainly one of these. Her story, what she's learned from it, and how she shares it, is nothing less than a gift to us all. When you are finished reading Terry's book, we suspect that like us, you'll close it, look up, and say "Thank you."

~ Drs. Ron and Mary Hulnick, Founding Faculty and Co-Directors, The University of Santa Monica

Spoke by Spoke is the kind of book that I like to read one chapter at a time . . . in the morning . . . in the stillness . . . with a warm mug of coffee. Anyone who is looking to find true joy and to let go of angst and anxiety should read this book. Terry Chase tells stories about LIVING that I can relate to . . . storics that will stick with me and remind me of my infinite choices and possibilities when bad thoughts come up. I will be sharing this book with my clients!

~ Wayne Herring, Life Coach for Business Owners and founder of Business Builder Camp

The intimate, raw, and sometimes shocking stories shared in *Spoke by Spoke* are offered, one senses, not so much because the author needs to tell them, but because she knows that we need to hear them; that we need to be encouraged and inspired and reminded, perhaps now more than ever, that after the darkest night, light returns; that we can do hard things; that even when we least expect it, hope and joy and love can move into our aching hearts and souls and bodies and make themselves at home, transforming our lives. What a gift—thank you!

~ **Janet F. Quinn, Ph.D., RN, FAAN,** Spiritual Director, author of *I Am a Woman Finding My Voice*

Terry Chase's *Spoke by Spoke* will touch your heart and give you new hope for humanity's capacity to change and grow in the face of the most abrupt and life-threatening challenges. A huge source of inspiration!

~ **Steve Chandler,** author of *Time Warrior*

When I read *Spoke by Spoke* the word that immediately came to mind was triumph. This is a story about triumph and finding great victory in the midst of life's toughest challenges. Dr. Terry Chase invites us into her own inspiring journey of self discovery and allows us to see that the real victory is the one we find within ourselves. Terry is a miracle! She lives what she writes in these pages and has been an inspiration to me. After reading this book you will also be inspired and ready to create miracles in your own life while never looking at so-called challenges the same way again. In her own joyful, fun and creative way, Terry allows us to see that anything is possible if we keep learning, keep growing, and keep riding (horses in her case). If you are ready to uplevel every area of life and give up all your excuses to create an extraordinary life, this book is for you.

~ **Devon Bandison,** MPA, Personal & Business Coach

WOW, Dr. Terry Chase shares her incredibly powerful and

inspiring life story with us on each and every page. Her story is a reflection of all of our life stories—there is disappointment, pain, grief, frustration, anger, hope, inspiration, love, passion and, most of all, a lightness and laughter we can all learn from. A must read. Thank you for sharing your life with us, Terry.

~ **Tina Quinn,** Life & Leadership Coach, Speaker

Books written from the heart, lift hearts! During times of transformation, Terry's book will inspire the reader to live fully and thrive freely.

~ **Sandra Ford Walston,** The Courage Expert, author of *Courage: The Heart and Spirit of Every Woman* and *The Courage Difference at Work: A Unique Success Guide for Women*

If you are looking for a message to inspire an effort to overcome seemingly insurmountable challenges, this is it. Dr. Chase has written a memoir that will lift you to new heights and make you wonder how such *joie de vivre* can grow from tragedy.

~ **Steve ErkenBrack,** Former District Attorney, Former CEO, Rocky Mountain Health Plans

Many of us have challenges and unforeseen changes in our lives. Some people never recover fully. In this heartfelt and vulnerable story, Dr Terry Chase walks us along her road to recovery and inspiration. I am moved by the details of what it took to rebuild her life from the pavement up. The perseverance and courage required not only becoming adept at living in a wheelchair but also becoming a force of good and inspiration for others through her work as professional coach and leader. One of the great metaphors I will take into my life from the book is how to turn a crushed bike into a windchime and a symbol of freedom. *Spoke by Spoke* is for anybody who wants to connect with their own indomitable human spirit and emerge renewed and refreshed. I encourage you to savor the words and powerful messages in this beautiful true story of grit and grace.

~ **Stephen McGhee,** Leadership Coach and Founder of the L4 initiative

Clarity. Honesty. Gut-wrenching depth of feeling. Chase conveys hope, creativity and adaptability that is so powerful it genuinely makes me wish I WERE HER right now. This author is role model for the role models! She's got the secret—something all of us want. And need. Find out what.

~ **Sunny Roller, M.A.,** Polio Survivor, Author, University of Michigan, Research Assistant, Teacher, Program Innovator

A remarkable story told with humor, grit and grace. Terry is an inspiration to all who have experienced a life-changing challenge. People of all ages can draw much from her honesty and incredible capacity to grow out of brokenness.

~ **Dr. Lisa Jordan, RN, CNE,** Professor of Nursing

Dr. Terry Chase has written an uplifting and inspirational memoir of her journey after a spinal cord injury left her partially paralyzed. I felt like I was sitting at lunch with Terry and she was sharing the intimate details of her life. Her perseverance, grace, and humor shine through as she shares stories and lessons we can all benefit from. From her physical, emotional, and spiritual trials to "accepting the challenges and blessings as one," Terry shows us we can be anyone and accomplish anything, regardless of our circumstances. For anyone who believes their life is too difficult and who is seeking answers, Terry will show you how to create whatever your heart desires.

~ **Karen Davis,** Co-Author of *How to Get the Most Out of Coaching, A Client's Guide for Optimizing the Coaching Experience*

Spoke by Spoke, without a doubt, will motivate the reader to rethink life: its challenges, its losses, its milestones, and to make the right changes which gift us, and gift those around us too.

~ **Sandy Maguire,** Educator, Artist, blessed friend of the author

SPOKE by SPOKE

SPOKE by SPOKE

How a Broken Back and a Broken Bike
Led to a WholeHearted Life

TERRY CHASE, ND, MA, RN, CEIP-Ed

PUSH ON
PRESS

Spoke by Spoke: How a Broken Back and a Broken Bike Led to a WholeHearted Life

Push On Press
Grand Junction, Colorado

Contact the author: www.drterrychase.com

Editing: Chris Nelson

ISBN: 978-1-7378623-0-7

Library of Congress Control Number: 2021919249

First edition

Some names and identifying details of individuals in this book have been changed to protect their privacy.

To Sharon

You have loved me through it all.

Table of Contents

A Wholehearted Life:
One Step at A Time

I'm biking into Grand Junction, Colorado, crossing the Colorado River bridge on a fast-paced, ten-mile ride through a favorite route on the outskirts of town.

Out of nowhere, the big, black Lincoln Continental—driven by a drunk—slams into me, tossing my body onto its hot hood. I hear my bike being crumpled beneath the vehicle as I ride the hood of the speeding car until it swerves, at which point I roll off and hit the pavement—hard. The vehicle drives off. My broken bike and I lie helpless in the road.

My life is changed in an instant.

Strangers stop and call for emergency help. I ask a man in brown boots, "Where are my legs?"

Because I can't feel them.

I grip his boot as he replies, trying to be reassuring, "Right here on the ground."

The last sense I'd had of my legs was in the air as I fell to the pavement. But the man has told me the truth, something I will learn to value in the coming days, months and years. I already know this is going to be bad, and I have to find a way to ground myself. At this moment, I simply cling to this stranger's boot, breathless and scared.

Lights, sirens, emergency crews and police surround me. I'm loaded onto a stretcher for transport to the hospital. I watch as the police pick up my mangled bike and toss it into the trunk of the squad car, an evidence tag dangling from it.

"Hey guys," I say to the paramedics, my breaths shallow because of the pain in my back, "the pea-green ceiling of this ambulance is really boring. Maybe a picture or two would make it more interesting."

My back may be broken. My sense of humor is still intact.

What is Spoke by Spoke?

At the time of the accident I was an active thirty-two-year-old. The result of that day was a traumatic spinal cord injury, and now it's been over thirty years using a wheelchair and crutches for mobility. For most of those years I was not willing to identify myself as a person with a disability. I fought the labels, the low expectations, the inequities and the inaccessibility I encountered in our society. I wanted something more. I wanted a wholehearted life.

Early on, I made some very clear decisions and set strong intentions, determined to make this situation work to my advantage. I have lived a vigorous and transformed life. My wheelchair has been a gift. In this book I'll share my stories of learning in the hopes that I will inspire others living with challenges. I've been told that what I have accomplished in the thirty-plus years since my accident is remarkable, even for a fully functioning body. But for me it goes beyond simple accomplishment—it was about my quest to live fully and to thrive.

Basically, it's time to give back, and I offer this book as an act of service to help anyone move forward, take a step, do a do, love a love, live a life.

You may be dealing with disability, illness or limitations getting in the way of what you want. Possibly my stories will inspire and guide you to take steps towards creating your desired life. But I won't preach or demand. I want to inspire others, to help people choose life on their own terms, just as I did with myself after the accident.

I have also had plenty of help along my way too. Through my stories, you will meet some of those "angels" on earth who came to my aid when I needed them, and perhaps this will help you recognize some of the angels in your own life.

I've grown in all ways: mentally, emotionally, physically and certainly spiritually. My expanded outdoor repertoire now includes sea kayaking, handcycling, wheelchair tennis, waterskiing and cross-country skiing. I found a healing connection with horses, and they too have taught me so much. I've travelled the world, opened my mind and softened my heart. I discovered strength in weakness. I allowed love into my life. I came to know that paralysis isn't always or only of the body. It can also be of the mind and heart.

You will see that not all of my lessons were pleasant or fun, but they were certainly necessary for deeper understanding and growth. Ultimately, against all expected odds, my physical paralysis offered me the opportunity to become free. *Spoke by*

Spoke shares tales from my journey.

I have divided this book into three "spokes," or sections, each of which captures different aspects of the beginning, middle and most recent phases of my journey.

Spoke One contains several stories involving my initial adjustment to life with a spinal cord injury. It shares insights and experiences from my rehabilitation therapy and some very dark times during those early days. It was during this time that I found ways to shift back into my adventurous lifestyle with the support of guides, mentors and angels who showed up at the right times and became my saving graces.

Spoke Two offers glimpses into the process of accepting my changed body. Healing on many levels of my life was not an easy course. I discovered a pathway towards helping other people but learned I had to help myself first. My personal and professional superpowers were in their developmental stages of growth. The time I'd spent on the patient side of the bedrail supported my growing abilities on the other side—as a professional healthcare provider.

Spoke Three is a collection of stories and lessons learned from my time working with horses. The horses became my guides, my healers, and my companions. They helped me be a much better human being through their kindness, presence, and honesty.

I trust all these stories will inspire you to live your own wholehearted life too.

Spoke 1

1

Tough Call

"I can't make my summer assignments!" I cried to my Colorado Outward Bound School director. "I've been in an accident. I'm in the hospital and my legs are partially paralyzed."

I'd made that call from my hospital bed—probably the most difficult call so far in my adult life.

Outward Bound instructors lead a patrol of ten adolescent students up, over, and through the Colorado mountains—and beyond their self-perceived inner limitations. As part of that program, I taught mountaineering, rock climbing and self-discovery. I'd loved my four previous summers doing this work and had had the privilege of witnessing some incredible student growth and learning.

Now I was paralyzed and had to give it all up. It was devastating, to say the least.

"Of course, Terry," the director said, her voice full of deep caring and concern. "I'm so sorry for you. I want you to know Outward Bound will still be here for you when you're ready to return. There will always be a place for you in this school."

I took that as a challenge. One of my goals would be to return to Outward Bound, to once again help educate young people to literally and figuratively climb mountains. Now, I had my own mountain in front of me, my own lessons to learn along the way—and they would be as real as they were at 14,000 feet.

So I determined to adopt the philosophy of Outward Bound—*To serve, to strive and not to yield*—applying it and the metaphors of the mountains to my new challenges of living with spinal cord injury and navigating life from a wheelchair.

I approached each new challenge much as my young students would have when faced with their Outward Bound challenges: river crossings require scouting the banks for breaks and easier passage; climbing a rock face necessitates setting up and fully securing all the ropes and anchors along the various routes. Different levels of difficulty on the climbing routes offer tests of varying strength for the young students. As a mountain climber and Outward Bound instructor, I had traveled across canyons and ridges using topographic maps of altitude, distance and barriers along the way.

Now it was my turn to scout for the new edges, to look for breaks and easier crossings—from my wheelchair. I scanned parking lots for the easiest and safest routes through. Distracted drivers wouldn't have a clear view of me as I sat low in my chair, so I had to look for *them*. I learned to accurately estimate whether an opening was big enough for my chair so I wouldn't have to stop and ponder if my now twenty-two inches could make it through.

Transportation systems often presented just such challenges. One time I wanted to watch my partner Sharon run the Boston

Marathon. The subway systems in Boston offered a few stations along the marathon route that were wheelchair accessible. But I quickly found out that the two accessible subway entrances didn't even get me close to the course. So I pushed my chair along the route and found a diner with an accessible entrance and an available restroom, a fine vantage point for five hours of watching runners.

Each new challenge became a problem to be solved. Back in the late eighties and early nineties, maps for navigating in a wheelchair were nowhere to be found. So, I typically charted my own course. Today technology has come a long way, and there are smartphone apps directing users to accessible restaurants, wheelchair-friendly parks and flatter terrain for exploration.

I learned to take natural consequences into account, too, another lesson instilled in me from the Outward Bound program. Students on an OB course were taught that if a tent isn't set up correctly the wind will blow it down. Often they had to learn the hard way—getting caught in midnight storms and finding themselves outside, struggling to pull their tents back into place for protection against the mountain elements. Even simply learning to pack a backpack with heavier items balanced and tucked in properly became a skill, because it afforded a much more comfortable walk during the long days on the trail. In the same way, I now had to learn how to pace myself in my chair, to plan my routes considering timing, wheelchair obstacles and more.

What's more, I knew that if I didn't take care of my spinal cord-injured body, there would be natural consequences—further deterioration and the possibility that this body wouldn't be there for me for as long as it could be. So many changes to consider when the body is partially paralyzed! The alteration in sensation, muscle function, circulation and temperature regulation make it even more important to pay attention to what my body is trying to tell me.

I found a way forward in this journey, as I always had in Outward Bound. Only now, instead of analyzing each new rock face, river crossing and terrain type, I calculated how to use my wheelchair to navigate curbs, board a bus or attend graduate school with a determination to *serve* others, to *strive* beyond my limits and not to *yield*.

As you can imagine, there was a quite a learning curve.

2

Lighten Up

I was serious. Dead serious after this injury that took away my powerful legs and back muscles. No laughing, no lightness in my being. I was reading books about other catastrophic illnesses and injuries, hoping to find the way through this ordeal. I was looking for a miracle.

One of those books was *Love, Medicine & Miracles* by Bernie Seigel, a physician who wrote about healing, particularly for people who have cancer. I liked his message of hope in the midst of tragedy and suffering. I was suffering with my own dramatic change in my body's function, mobility and ease of movement.

One passage in particular stood out for me in the book: "Those with spinal cord injury who deal with their anger do better in life than those who do not."

I wasn't dealing with my anger. I was looking for the easy way out. Keeping it stuffed down was my usual way. Only now that anger was seeping out in all sorts of ways.

Then one night early in my rehab stay at Craig Hospital, the intercom speaker squawked with the voice of the unit secretary:

"Terry, there's someone here to see you. Are you okay with her coming to your room for a short visit?"

"I'm busy reading tonight," I said, slightly irritated by the interruption. "Can you tell me who it is? A name, maybe?"

"It's Sharon Blackburn," the secretary said, as if I was supposed to know who that was.

"I don't know who that is," I said, feeling resigned, "but go ahead and have her come to my room for a minute." I was attempting to be polite, but it was a stretch for me at that moment.

Shortly after this a woman whom I'd never met walked into the room. She was smiling, healthy-looking and athletic. I would come to know she had recently completed the Ironman Triathlon in Hawaii, and biking was her favorite sport.

"Hi, Terry," Sharon said. "I'm a friend of your friend Karen from Grand Junction. We know each other from softball. She asked if I'd come over and say hello. I just happened to be in the building tonight. How are you?" She didn't show any evidence of discomfort about the fact that I was in a hospital bed, surrounded with tubes and all kinds of medical equipment.

I mumbled a few words about being "okay," and then she went on without pause, "Did you know there's a talent show going on in the gym? How come you're not down there? A friend of mine—a former patient—is the emcee for the show."

This Sharon Blackburn is a talker, I thought to myself.

"Well, I'm in bed reading a book," I said with some consternation at this woman's obvious inability to see that I happened to have a broken back and paralyzed legs.

She remained undaunted by my protest that reading a serious book about serious injuries and illnesses was more important than going to a talent show in a hospital gymnasium. *And the talent would be other patients?* I thought to myself. *Really? That's a show?*

"I'll just stay here for tonight," I said, slightly gritting my teeth. "Maybe another time, but thanks for asking." She was starting to make me even more angry than I'd been before she came into the room.

But at the same time there was also something so very touching and sweet about her that I couldn't just tell her to go.

This woman whom I did not know and who was simply a friend of a friend now made herself comfortable in my room. She noticed some other books on my counter that my friends back home had sent me.

"These are funny," she said, holding up one for me to look at: *Tales of the City and More Tales of the City* by some guy named Armistead Maupin. "Have you read these?"

"No," I said, still feeling a little irritated. "I'm reading this book by Bernie Siegel."

Making herself even more comfortable in the chair, she began to read some of the passages by Maupin out loud, laughing and smiling as she did so. In spite of myself I began to loosen up too. Something about her presence made me start feeling more comfortable with myself. My defenses were beginning to drop.

It happened pretty quickly. For some reason—maybe because there was no hesitancy from her and she seemed quite comfortable with me—soon I didn't feel I had to hide my deficits under the thin white hospital sheets. The wheelchair placed by my bedside was not a hindrance and she looked straight into my eyes. I felt it was okay to be vulnerable; she saw the real me, despite my trying to cover it up.

After a little while she paused and said, "Well, maybe you'll want to read these. They may help lighten you up a bit during this rehab thing." She said this with what seemed to me an immense amount of seriousness and compassion.

That invitation to "lighten up a bit" was the most helpful thing anyone had yet said to me in rehab.

I was serious. I always had been, and certainly at that terrible time in my life I was *profoundly* serious. Yet my seriousness did not deter her. She made me laugh after making me angry. She took the time to connect with me, and risked suggesting I might want to lighten up a bit.

It was just what I needed.

The back story on this was that Sharon was a physical therapist who had been working at Craig for a few years and decided to take a break from rehabilitation and work in an orthopedic clinic. She wanted to get a taste of another experience as a Physical Therapist. She loved Craig Hospital and its mission and service to people with catastrophic spinal cord and brain injuries. And, she jumped at any chance she got to come back into that building with *those people*. That evening of the talent show was her opportunity to reconnect with a former patient and meet me.

It was an opportunity for me, too.

The encounter was the beginning of our three-decade-long relationship. What began as friendship in that hospital room turned into a romantic and loving partnership. Sharon met me at the most vulnerable point of my life. It didn't matter to her that I was paralyzed and broken. She shared my love of biking, being outdoors—and black dogs. I shared my humorous side with her, and she appreciated my dry wit even during pain and sorrow.

With her, I began to laugh again.

I lightened up—exactly what I needed to do for the long journey ahead.

3

Is it a Crying Day or Laughing Day?

Most early mornings in the hospital began with the warm, smiling face of Earl the Pearl—my rehab tech—peeking through the opening of the flimsy curtain in my hospital room, always smiling, always ready to receive whatever I had to give.

"Miss Terry," she'd ask, "is this a crying day or a laughing day?"

"I don't know, Earl," I'd solemnly reply. "I'll figure it out as we get going."

For the record, most of those early days were crying days. The tears kept coming, sometimes with no real reason. They just flowed. I was in a hospital with partially paralyzed legs that were no longer powerful enough to carry me up a mountainside or pedal a bike or chase my middle-school kids across a soccer field. Shadow, my beloved black lab, no longer had me to run with on our favorite three-mile course—which had kept us both in shape.

To gain some insight on my cycles of up and (mostly) down emotions, I turned to books about people with chronic illness and severe injury. Books had always been my solace, and now these gave me some new perspectives with which to approach this sudden change in my life. One common theme was that the anger and turbulent emotions that accompany sudden injury are to be expected. Repressing those emotions is detrimental to recovery—both physically and mentally—and only leads to more problems.

In other words, I learned that I had permission to feel sadness and anger, and, more importantly, to cry—but also to eventually let it go.

Earl the Pearl could handle whoever greeted her on the other side of the curtain—crying Terry or laughing Terry. Her cheerful face and caring eyes kept me safe. With her daily dose of kindness, there was no judgement and no expectation that I should be handling my situation in any particular way. She understood that the patient beyond the curtain might be having a difficult time. Whatever the emotion of the day, it was alright. She was there to do her job, and she showed up ready and willing.

I needed to show up too. My job was to get out of bed, get myself to meals, participate in therapy and learn about life in my wheelchair. Day in and day out, Earl the Pearl helped me do this. I had to get on with life, even the mundane and usual things like eating, brushing teeth, dressing, toileting and mobility. It was that simple. Do the usual stuff of life, and life will get better. There was no opening of the heavens, no brilliant internal flash that helped me in those early, dark days. I couldn't just wait for my body to suddenly heal or for the paralysis to go away. I couldn't wait for divine intervention to instantly transform me back to my pre-accident condition. I had to get moving with what was available to me at the time.

Whether it was a laughing day or a crying day, I chose to be kind. Earl the Pearl didn't have to put up with any disrespect or meanness from me. She let me know in her own, kind way that the routine of the day was to get up and get going. She let me pick out the shirt, shorts and socks for the day, then put them within my reach on the bed. I worked to dress myself, however slowly and clumsily at first. She went about her usual business—picking up dirty cups, emptying the trash, refreshing my towels and bedclothes—always keeping a watchful eye. She'd laugh and talk about her life too. Her children getting bigger, a husband who worked long hours. Together they provided a happy home for their family.

At times she would fall quiet and look at me with warmth as I struggled. I knew she knew this was hard. And that for me this struggle to get dressed was as important as those therapy exercises in the gym.

I had to learn.

I had to push through even when it seemed impossible.

Over the weeks, I got stronger, smarter and more efficient doing the commonplace activities of life. I could transfer out of the bed, grab those clothes, dress and be ready with a cleaned-up room before she'd even peek through the curtain. I surprised her. Some days I even surprised myself.

Is it a crying day or a laughing day? I know now that whether I was crying or laughing didn't matter. I just needed to *show up*. Letting the tears and the laughter out was how the healing began. I'd figured out that holding things in, stuffing them down, would only steal away my life energy.

I wanted to live.

I wanted my life to go on.
Laughing or crying—either way.

4

She Listened

After a long day of rehabilitation therapy, I pushed myself back to the hospital room and pressed the call button for help from the staff. I was tired. I felt heavy in the wheelchair that day. My current situation, the fatigue of small, tired muscles and the uncertainty of my future pressed me deeper into the wheelchair. It was time to get out of my clothes and shoes and stretch out a bit before dinner.

About ten minutes later, a rehab tech came into the room. He was a young guy, and something in his demeanor immediately said he didn't want to be there. The first words that came out of his mouth were, "You're lazy."

"What?" I said quickly, surprised and stung by his words. Being lazy was the farthest thing from my mind on any day, much less one in which I had been pushed to my limits physically, mentally and emotionally. Aside from the demanding exercise regimen, I was still dealing with the fact that I'd would probably be stuck pushing this wheelchair for the rest of my life.

I said, "I'm really tired. I just want a little help getting ready for the evening."

"Alright," he said. "What do you want me to do?"

This gruff, uncaring response was far from the usual treatment I got from the hospital staff. I felt a change come over me. It was like a slow boil building. The grip on my wheel rims tightened and I fixed my gaze on the wall ahead. My breathing became shallow, almost stopping.

"You know, never mind," I said abruptly. "I'm okay for now. Leave me alone."

He shrugged and promptly left the room.

So I sat. And sat. And sat. All through the evening, through the dinner hour, foregoing food. I never left the room, never asked for anything for the many hours to come. The wheelchair I hated became my sinking ground, holding me. I didn't know what was going on in my mind, but whatever it was, I knew it wasn't like me. This guy didn't know me. His stinging, unkind comments had paralyzed me even more.

The late afternoon sun settled into sundown, and soon the sky outside the hospital window was dark.

There was a knock on the door and Cathy, the evening shift nurse, came in. "What's up, Terry? I haven't seen you out of your room tonight." She pulled up a chair and sat down next to me, but I remained silent. "This isn't like you. What's going on?"

I shifted and looked up as a heavy sigh escaped my sunken chest. I had been crying. My body felt especially frail and fragile.

I hesitated before speaking. "I don't want to get anyone in trouble," I said, "but that rehab tech told me I was lazy when I asked for help." I was both irritated and sad. "I am *not* lazy! I hate asking for help. I wouldn't ask for help if I didn't really need it."

Something within me broke and the tears began again. I had been pushed to my limit. The tech's words were the equivalent of being kicked when I was already down.

I leaned forward into the outstretched arms of the nurse.

I had never been good at expressing emotions, even before the accident. I'd kept them bottled up. That day, I did it again—after a day of grueling therapy work, I focused and pushed aside emotions. And when evening arrived, I was *still* holding on to those overwhelming feelings of frustration and sadness and helplessness.

But when the nurse reached out to me, that was all it took— that simple expression of support and compassion—to make the dam inside me break open. The emotion flooded through me and I cried and cried.

The nurse held me while the emotions flowed.

After a while, I said, "I hate being paralyzed! I want to just get up and leave, but I can't! This stupid wheelchair is my only way to get around. I'm stuck here and I'm too tired to do anymore." The words rushed out. "I work so hard and I'm still weak. And I don't *like* asking for help. I'm used to being independent. That rehab tech makes me so angry I'll hit the wall or spit at him if he ever comes near me again!"

My grip on the rims of the wheels loosened as the tension started to ebb away.

The nurse said, "Terry, I know for a fact you're not even close to lazy. It's the last way I think of you. Let's get you out of those clothes, and I'll get that pink basin of hot water and a soapy cloth so you can wash up. The kitchen still has some fried chicken and mashed potatoes from dinner. I'll get a plate ready." She was about to stand up when she added, "Oh, and here are your meds for tonight," as she handed over the med cup. "Is there anything else you want to talk about?"

I felt a new kind of lightness as I sat up in the wheelchair. "No, I'm good. Thanks for listening."

As I look back today, many years later, I'm certain that Cathy was one of several incredible nurses who inspired me to become a nurse myself. Cathy knew how to take care of me as a person, not just as a patient. She was kind. She knew how to make me laugh, even when things weren't going great. She also knew how and when to get down to business.

Most importantly, she listened when I needed to be heard.

I've carried this lesson from Cathy forward into my own work as a nurse, a teacher, and a coach. To be with someone in their time of pain, just listening and holding space, is healing and transformative.

5

A Plain, White Garment

Saturday, late afternoon. I'm sitting in a wheelchair in my rehab hospital room. I've just returned from an outing to the shopping mall. This wheelchair and I are getting to know each other a little better. Recreation therapy outings are designed to help patients new to spinal cord injuries and wheelchairs navigate the world again. Malls aren't my usual environment for weekend adventures, but I'd sign up for *anything* to get out of the hospital. On this particular outing, I'd rolled along the smooth, wide mall hallways and maneuvered through racks of summer dresses and stacks of packaged underwear. At the food court, I'd purchased a soda and a hot dog—passing the test of handling myself, my money and the wheelchair under the watchful eye of a recreation therapist.

Now the day is done and it's time to make the transfer to my hospital bed. I still require the supervision of a nursing orderly to ensure I get from wheelchair to bed without ending up on the floor.

I press the call button and politely say to the ward clerk on the other end of the speaker, "Okay, I'm ready for a transfer. Can you send in an orderly, please?"

I am a compliant rehab patient for the most part. Yet there are some rules I break on purpose. For example, I won't sign back into the patient logbook when returning from an out-of-hospital experience. It's my little bit of rebellion as a grown woman under the supervision of hospital workers.

I wait for the orderly. I've come to know that workers don't always respond all that fast; there are many other patients and potential interruptions on their way to my room. So I get used to waiting, and that's what I do now. I sit and wait. And I wait some more.

A light knock on the door gets my attention. This is a bit unusual; the orderlies usually just bust in without much warning, so I'm surprised someone is bothering to knock.

"Come on in! I'm decent," I say with a wry smile on my face, my modesty long since tempered from having been in the hospital for a couple of months.

"Oh, hi." The words come from a small-statured, grey-haired woman I've never seen before. She's very non-descript and plain looking, and she walks slowly and softly into my room, almost as if she's tiptoeing. Something is . . . different about her. I can't recall having seen her before.

"I am ——." She gives me a name I don't recognize (and which I still can't remember).

"Uh, hello," I say. "How can I help you?" This seems like a reasonable response to a situation that feels slightly odd. Maybe she's lost, or looking for my roommate.

She holds a white shirt in her arms, apparently offering it to me. I sit still, wondering what exactly is happening. All my clothes are neatly stacked in the hospital room closet; nothing is missing, as far I know. Certainly not this white shirt.

"You have been blessed by this circumstance," she says in what I can only describe as a soft, loving voice. "There are many great things ahead if you are willing to accept the blessings. I have brought you a garment, a symbol of this new life for you."

This all feels rather . . . strange. I'm Catholic-educated and a regular participant in Mass, so I can appreciate the mystical in the world, even ideas about spirits and unseen influences. I'm not even afraid of or weirded-out by her comment. In fact, I feel fully present in this moment of exchange, so much so that it feels charged with something other-worldly.

She stands still, extending the garment to me. I sit there silently, not knowing what to do. Should I hit that buzzer again? Should I be afraid even though I don't feel it? I don't know this lady, and I want to believe I don't have any idea what she's talking about. Yet on another level I am listening intently, as if understanding something on some other level than what I'm aware of.

The shirt she's holding out to me is a thigh-length pullover, a few buttons, no zippers. It doesn't bear any store tags or labels. It's just a plain, white garment with simple embroidery along the neckline—a very "homemade" look.

"Okay," I say at last, with a little bit of skepticism and, perhaps, curiosity. I had decided early on that this accident was a kind of spiritual wake-up call. I would use it as an opportunity for growth and a new direction. I just wasn't expecting anyone *else* to know of my thoughts on the subject—not least some random stranger in my hospital room. I take the garment from her outstretched hands and lay it on my lap.

And just as quickly as she entered my room, she exits . The white garment lies across my lap. My mind and heart are touched by this brief encounter , which I really don't even understand.

The door immediately swings open again. "Okay!" says the orderly who bursts in. "Ready for that transfer?"

"Sure," I reply. "Hey, do you know that lady? The one who just left my room as you came in?"

"Nope," he says casually, focusing on the task at hand. "Didn't see anyone. Ready?" He helps me up over the wheel of my chair and into the bed, then straightens out my legs, removes my shoes and pulls a sheet over me. The mysterious white garment is hung up in the closet without a word.

***

For many years I never told anyone about the woman's visit or the garment she gave me. Not the nurses, not the doctor, not even a counselor who helped me during the dark times. I still have the garment—it's in my closet as I write this. And I still vividly remember that day way back in 1988. That visit from a kind stranger, a white garment so unique, and a message to accept the challenges and blessings as one.

I hold that memory close to my heart. Maybe the lady was an angel or some other type of spiritual being—or maybe she was just someone with a kind nature who randomly walked into hospital rooms and handed out white shirts. I don't know.

But I *do* agree with her that my spinal cord injury and my sudden change in life direction held blessings I could never have imagined. This brief exchange and the acceptance of the garment, as well as the accompanying message, became a touchstone for my life with spinal cord injury.

6

Three Little Lessons from a Tennis Ball

May I be completely honest with you? Tennis was not a sport I liked, much less played. But the college requirements for becoming a physical education teacher included not only passing intermediate tennis but also demonstrating an ability to *teach* tennis. I duly followed through and completed the course, but once done with college I thought I'd never pick up a racquet again. I never played tennis with my middle-school students, and never watched a tennis match.

But then the unexpected happened, and I learned quite a lot from a little tennis ball.

Get Up and Go Play

It was a couple of months into my rehab program. I had become independent in transfers and needed much less help from the nursing staff. One evening Paula, my rehab hospital roommate, said to me, "I'm going down to the gym to try wheelchair tennis. Want to go with me?"

"I'm alright," I replied sleepily from my hospital bed. "Go ahead. I'll catch up with you later." I was tired at the end of a busy day of rehabilitation. Learning new wheelchair skills, therapy sessions and practicing the activities of daily living left me with little energy, especially for a sport I didn't like.

I know what you're thinking: "She's an athlete! A PE teacher! A sports enthusiast!" All true. I had played on the college softball team as a walk-on. Just picked up the bat at tryouts and hit a long fly ball. After that, the third base position (lots of action here) was my spot for four years on scholarship. I also loved peddling my bike on long country road rides.

I was no stranger to the physical and mental efforts of being an athlete. But none of that was enough to get me out of bed and onto the court that evening. So I continued to lie there.

Then it hit me. My roommate didn't even look athletic. She was a bit clumsy, often dropping things off her bedside table. I might be disabled, but athleticism was part of my identity—something I still felt strongly.

My competitive streak kicked in and I thought, "If Paula's trying wheelchair tennis, then so am I." *That* was enough to spur me on. I could at least make a reluctant appearance.

I transferred out of bed and pushed down to the hospital gymnasium.

"Try it, Terry," said Carol, the recreation therapist. She presented me with a tennis racquet and further words of encouragement. "You've done other sports. I'm sure you'll pick this one up no problem at all."

"Okay, I'll give it try," I replied, halfheartedly at best.

I rolled my wheelchair out onto the basketball court (now doubling as a tennis court). I had to hold a racquet and push at the same time. Awkward wasn't even close to how this felt. I had barely learned to push that stupid wheelchair by itself, and now I had to do it with a racquet in my hand. I reach my position on the court, stopped the chair and held the wheels in place while bouncing the yellow ball at the side of the chair. I bounced the ball one last time and took a swing, felt that familiar feeling of the ball hitting the strings, heard the *thwack* of the ball and the sound of it striking the court on the other side of the net...

I tried again. I hit the first ball, then a second ball and again another ball. And just like that a light bulb went on in my head. "I can do this sport," I thought, surprised. "I'm hitting tennis balls! I'm in a wheelchair hitting tennis balls, and *I'm having fun!*"

***

Those were the humble beginnings of my sixteen-year wheelchair tennis career competing on the circuit, playing in men's and women's divisions, singles or doubles—it didn't matter. Just get me on the court!

When I returned to teaching physical education five months after the accident, wheelchair tennis became my go-to activity in the gym. I was back playing with the middle-school kids. Local tennis clubs donated old racquets, balls and nets, and I set up short courts in the gym. I modified the rules so that even the most challenged kid would find success in our games.

And so my teaching repertoire expanded to include a sport I'd never really liked before the accident. It helped me discover new ways to have fun and encourage my students. Tennis reduced the restrictions of a wheelchair and allowed me to grow in confidence as a PE teacher. I got to teach the way I loved: show, tell, and then *let's play!* Most importantly, we all forgot about the wheelchair, and I learned a few key lessons along the way.

Don't take it personally

Ever take something personally? I know what that feels like.

Every point scored against me in matches became a personal assault of sorts, shattering my game. I got so wrapped up in the game on the *other* side of the net that I lost control of what was happening on *my* side. I ended up playing into the opponent's game. They called the shots and I just chased them.

Until I *got it*. Somehow one day it hit me that I had to let go of taking each point so personally and let my own game come forward. I was a good player—if I let myself play. This meant accepting that I would be scored against now and then; that, after all, is how the game is played. I score. They score. Eventually the points add up to a winner. I had to play all-out to the final point, not get bogged down in each one along the way. That only made me lose *more* points.

I quit taking everything personally. It doesn't work on the tennis court, and it certainly doesn't work in life.

Expletives don't belong on the tennis court

"!@#$%^&*," I shouted, wheeling back to the baseline after a terrible shot. For emphasis I smacked the fence with my racquet.

Then something—or rather, someone—caught my eye. My

elderly grandmother was shuffling past on her way back from the restroom. Grandma Mooney didn't look at me. Never said a word. She didn't have to. All my embarrassment came from *me* as I suddenly saw through her eyes how I must have looked and sounded during my little tantrum. I was totally ashamed and schooled at the same time.

Shouting expletives on the tennis court ended abruptly that day. No more taking frustrations out on the fence and no more shouting curse words into the air. I knew this was bad behavior. I was not proud of it. Not only was it embarrassing, it also didn't help one bit. If anything, what I realized was that it undermined my confidence and ability to play the game.

Here's how I used my "tennis ball theory of learning: Pick up a tennis ball. Find the seam. It's usually white, a little rubber pathway around the ball. Put a dot on it: that's your starting point. Follow the seam with your finger while thinking about the process of learning something new. It certainly doesn't have to be tennis. Maybe it's a new hobby, a musical instrument, something to do with personal growth. Trace your finger along the path of the seam, pausing occasionally to think of the details of what you'll be learning, the surprises and wonders along the way. Say you're learning a new language. First you'll learn some vocabulary. Then how to put it into a sentence. Then how to actually communicate with someone else. But keep moving along that seam. Soon you'll be back to the starting place. And what do you find?

You're still on the path; learning never ends. And you keep growing the whole time.

***

I'm still amazed at all I've learned just because I dragged myself out of bed that day in rehab to play a sport I didn't even like.

7

Something Remarkable

I'd achieved the many goals rehab was designed to help me with. I could sit up and transfer myself—independently—from bed to wheelchair and back again. I could shower and get dressed. I felt like I was coming into my own again. The metal brace holding my spine erect would come off soon.

Fifty days into my stay, and discharge was only a week away.

What had really saved my sanity during this tough rehab stint was being introduced to opportunities for exercise and recreation by the Therapeutic Recreation Department. This was vital for me. Until recently I'd been an active, athletic woman, and I needed to once again feel those competitive juices flowing through my veins. It was this spirit that kept me going during those days of rehab.

And now I was cleared to go waterskiing.

I was so excited that I barely slept the night before. Tuesday morning, I was up early and ready for the morning bus ride to Boulder Reservoir. The nurses buzzed about me, making sure I got my medications and that my personal care was completed. I transferred myself slowly out of bed and into my wheelchair, grabbed a sweatshirt and headed out the door. The specially equipped activity bus left at 0600 sharp for the forty-mile road trip. I had a quick coffee and a snack for breakfast.

The lake was picture-perfect still, no ripples or wind. It was empty, too, all ours. No other boats were allowed for these weekly adaptive waterski sessions provided by the Boulder EXPAND Program for People with Disabilities.

Several people helped me prep. I was dressed only in shorts, a t-shirt, neoprene foot booties and a life vest, which was snug and secure. Then I took a short roll down the steep ramp to the gently swaying dock, which floated on the surface of the water. A special waterski awaited me: a plastic, one-piece office chair bolted to two wide waterskis. One end of the tow rope was attached to the chair, the other to the ski boat.

All-in-all it was an appropriate waterski setup for a new paraplegic from Craig Hospital.

I transferred from my wheelchair to the waterski; it was just like shifting from my wheelchair into a bed. My feet were tucked gently under a broad strap to keep them from bouncing out. Once settled into the seat, the next step became a rude, early morning wakeup: I was lowered slowly into the water, which was still cold from the night before. Helpers turned me to face the back of the boat and make sure I stayed upright in the water.

By now a morning breeze had risen and the boat bobbed gently in the rippling water. The boat's driver waited, steady and ready, for my shout.

"Hit it!" I cried, and the boat bolted forward, quickly gaining speed. The makeshift waterski abruptly gained momentum, and in a flash I was pulled up and out of the water.

I was waterskiing! The morning air and cold-water spray woke me up instantly. I held on tight, watching the lake scenery go by in fast motion.

I made it two full laps around the reservoir in seemingly no time at all. My face hurt from all the laughing and smiling. Before long the chill of the morning air was replaced with the warmth of the Colorado sunshine.

This outing became my "claim to fame," because I was waterskiing even before my discharge from the rehab hospital. And for many years afterwards I continued waterskiing with the Boulder Expand Program. My skills and confidence increased, and I could gradually switch to a less cumbersome adaptive waterski. I held my own rope for take-offs, and many times I didn't need the assistance of the chase boat to get back up because I never fell over or lost control on the rough waters. My goal was to complete two laps of the reservoir, make a perfect drop at the dock and be back on deck with my hair still dry.

Waterskiing wasn't just waterskiing. It was an opportunity to work through many of the difficult struggles associated with a spinal cord injury. The challenges of timing my shout of "Hit it!" while remaining steady in the water; of handling the deep wake rollers; of coming back week after week to gain greater strength and confidence in the sport—all of this tested me in ways that mirrored my struggles in other areas of my life, both physical and mental. So many times I'd take my life frustrations out on the lake, slapping the water in anger and working through the untold issues of living with a disability. I somehow knew that if I could handle the waters of Boulder Reservoir, I could handle the stresses of just about anything else.

And in a very real way, this has turned out to be true.

8

Roadside

I've got to pee.

Is it safe for me to pull over to the side of the road? Or should I wait to find a parking lot?

I've *really* gotta go . . . I can't hold it much longer. Feels like my bladder is going to burst.

If I don't pull over soon, I'll be wet for the duration of this long road trip. This thought makes the panic rise up, and combined with my urge to *go* it begins to overtake my ability to drive safely, because I'm frantically looking for the right place to stop—someplace protected from onlookers in passing cars, just far enough away from the road to keep anyone from accidentally running into me, and on a slight downhill-sloping angle so the pee rolls away under my vehicle.

Suddenly I see it: the right place.

I glance around—is anyone watching?

Nope. All clear.

I stop the car, shift to park, open the door, swing my legs out, lean myself against the car frame, undo belt and zipper, pull pants down just below my bottom area, and answer the call of my bladder.

Relief at last.

Peeing roadside can be dangerous, and not just in terms of getting into an accident. There's also the possibility of being seen by a passerby, or worse, noticed by a cop who has a problem with public urination and is ready to ticket. It hasn't happened yet, but if a cop ever wants to ask, I have my story ready just in case:

"Officer, I'm sorry I have to pee here. It's either this or I'll wet my pants, and that would be uncomfortable and unhealthy. I promise I'll plan better next time."

Hopefully I'll never have to use that explanation.

I'm also very careful never to pee near a school or playground, or anywhere else children might be nearby. The last thing I want is to traumatize some young mind or be mistaken for a pervert.

The fact is, it's not always a simple matter of planning ahead. My demanding bladder and its immediate needs are related to my spinal cord injury. I've gotten to know my bladder quite well over the past thirty years since the injury, and we've developed a relationship based on trust and honest communication. But it's still challenging. Most people unfamiliar with the details of a spinal cord injury (SCI) assume that loss of muscle function and the inability to walk are the worst consequences. And there's no denying that these are obvious challenges. But more hidden losses, like bladder control, are real struggles as well. One result of damaged spinal cord tissue can be that the signals going to and from the bladder are interrupted; normal sensation and function are off-line, so to speak. The same can happen with other important spots in the pelvic area, such as the bowels. Sexual functioning can take a hit as well.

These hidden losses can be extremely challenging both physically and emotionally, and especially in terms of self-esteem and self-confidence. Usually the last time most people discuss bathroom routines is around age two during potty-training. Once we know the drill, we're left alone to take care of business behind closed doors.

But the losses associated with SCI open a person to a new kind of invasion of privacy, one where important and usually private physical functions have to be discussed openly with healthcare providers. Individuals with SCI typically have to be instructed in new routines for dealing with basic bodily needs. Modesty goes out the window. The newly injured person is forced to relearn essential functions using foreign objects like catheters and leg-bags. Fortunately, my own bladder has enough function preserved to allow freedom from using such items. But I have challenges too.

A few years after my spinal injury cord, I applied to nursing school, a rigorous graduate program that would require four years and 4,000 clinical hours to complete. I was concerned that my injury and the use of a wheelchair would be seen as a detriment to participating in classes and clinical rotations. I was also concerned about my erratic bladder behavior. I could handle the academics and demanding schedule; I just wasn't sure how the other parts of my body would behave under that kind of stress.

As part of the application process I was granted an interview with the Dean of the Nursing program. I wanted to show my capability by walking into the interview using crutches instead of a wheelchair. This approach—using forearm crutches, and braces on my lower legs—was a major effort and not the most efficient way of getting around, but on this occasion I stood tall, pushed myself hard—and made it look easy. I hoped this display would leave no doubt about my ability to keep up with and succeed in the program.

The hour-long session in the dean's office went well. I was pleased and comfortable with our heartfelt and sincere dialogue about my wishes for nursing as a new career. When the interview was complete, I stood up, shook her hand, and expressed my desire to be honored with acceptance into this great nursing program.

Then my bladder gave me that familiar call.

In times of high emotion and stress my bladder is often more demanding. This was one of those times. Nursing interview or no nursing interview, I had to pee *immediately*. I made it to the front desk, said goodbye to the dean, exchanged niceties with the administrative assistant . . . all the while walking slowly backward through the office suite, hoping they would not see the streak of wet going down the inner thighs of my light-green slacks. (I was accepted to the program—and never, ever told the dean why I walked backward out of her office suite that day.)

That wasn't the last day that my self-esteem took a blow— this time below the belt. There were many more days ahead when I wet myself and there was nothing I could do. I always kept clean, dry clothes ready just in case.

I still locate the bathroom first thing whenever I visit a new building, shopping center or recreation setting. My reconnaissance includes estimating time and distance to the bathroom, determining how easy it will be to open the door and counting the number of handicap stalls, all so that I have a plan when my bladder emits that familiar signal.

I'm rather lucky. I do have enough sensation and reliable function to know when it's time and just how long I can hold it before all bets are off. Many factors can mess up this slight advantage, however. I can drink one too many cups of coffee in a day, enjoy a large glass of orange juice or eat cool watermelon slices, all of which have diuretic effects on the body and increase the need to urinate. I always have to be aware of intake and its potential effect on output.

I approach this area of my life with great planning and care. It is still humiliating to pee my pants. At best there are times when I just have sit in it and wait it out . . . like during a tennis match, or teaching a class. I wear protective pads of all sizes and capability to accommodate the need. This is something I have learned to do over the years—there weren't as many options for incontinence capture when I first got hurt. I also have some techniques to calm my bladder; sometimes they work and other times not so much. I rock in the chair; scoot forward and sometimes rub my leg to get the attention off the sensation in my bladder and onto another part of my body. Nothing is fool-proof, however, and I usually rush into the bathroom stall or out the door of my vehicle to release the increasing discomfort.

I have many more bladder adventures to share, but I'll stop for now…

My bladder is calling.

9

Three White Bellies

Eight brightly colored, plastic sea kayaks bobbed in the gentle sea surf off the coast of Washington state. We were venturing through the waters around the San Juan Islands, a small group of explorers lined up side by side, silently watching and waiting for orcas. This was day two of a three-day adventure. The "orca day" was the most anticipated event of this short sea kayak excursion and the main reason why most of us signed up for this trip in early July, midway through the April to October migration season of the mighty orca whales.

We arrived at our spot after a short paddle around the coves and shorelines of San Juan Island. Now it was mid-afternoon, just the right time to set up, watch and wait. Tim, the burly, sun-soaked trip leader, said to the group, "I've been out on these waters for sixteen years, and those orcas never disappoint me. I just don't know exactly when or where the whales will show up. But if they *do,* we're in the best place to see them."

Anticipatory giggles and excited laughter rose up from the group members, but small talk was kept to a minimum as we sat facing west, rising and falling gently in the swells of the cold Pacific waters. All eight kayaks were backed up against a steep granite rock wall that plunged straight into the water—no sandy shoreline here—and nestled amidst the tangle of seaweed and long strands of kelp that rose up from the bottom. We were at what was considered a safe distance for viewing, about a quarter of a mile away from the whales' highway.

"Look! There they are!" shouted a young woman from Chicago in a red kayak.

Three hundred yards ahead of us, streaming across the open water on their way north, the sleek backs of orcas started breaking the surface of the water. Soon the sea was full of the massive black-and-white bodies, blowing air and snorting sea water, moving swiftly along. Within the pod they seemed to move in groups of three, four, five. Sometimes a single whale would rise up majestically, its slippery skin shining in the sun, then dip back beneath the water.

Clicks and whirrs from cameras filled the air. I raised my own camera to my eye and followed the stream of life before me, trying to click with intention but never really knowing when a whale might pop up or blow a geyser of water into the air. My stomach was doing flip-flops, my breath quickening.

Here I was, far away from my wheelchair, sitting in a sea kayak on the edge of the Pacific Ocean. Three hundred yards away these massive, glistening giants rose and fell in majestic rhythm as they migrated north, in tune with some ancient drive to survive.

My kayak was positioned at the far end of our line; to my left was open water. As I sat there, mesmerized by the whales, my gaze shifted out across the water and I noticed that a small group of whales had broken away from their northward route and were heading east—directly towards the kayak line-up. At first I simply kept taking pictures—what else could I do? But as they kept coming I felt a rush of energy, an overwhelming feeling of, "Oh, shit! Now what?"

I quickly realized I was the only one in our group who saw the whales coming—everyone else was still gazing at the main line of whales. So I yelled, "Look to your left! Orcas are coming at us!"

The three big black-and-white bodies, fins above water, powered directly toward our kayaks. I kept snapping pictures, not wanting to miss a single shot. Before they even reached this line up of kayaks, I felt the swell of water generated by their bodies beneath the surface. Just before they reached us the three orcas—possibly a papa, mama and baby—all turned belly up. Then these three tuxedo bellies swiftly darted under our boats, heaving us up in one gigantic wave. At that moment I didn't even think of the danger—what would have happened if any part of those gleaming torsos struck my boat? What if their powerful tails slapped at just the wrong moment and slammed into the fragile plastic of my kayak?

But all my focus was on snapping pictures. There was no fear, just a sense of wonder. And then they were gone, back out to sea, absorbed into the pod, cruising the busy orca highway.

Not a single boat was overturned. Not one person hurt. It was all over in a flash of a second, and I was left wondering, "Why did they do this? What made them break off from the main line of traffic and divert to where our kayaks were all lined up near a wall of granite in a supposedly protected location?"

It was not until the next day, while looking through the photos I had taken during the event—seeing in freeze-frame the three black fins and large bodies coming at me, the white bellies sliding beneath my boat—did I really realize the power of that moment. Those whales could have wiped us out with one flick of a tail. If they'd chosen at that moment to rise for a breath of air they would've tossed us and our boats out of the water like bowling pins.

This potential for serious injury in a collision of whales and plastic kayaks hung heavy on my mind for days and weeks to come. Even now, many years later I realize how in an instant I could have been hurt badly, perhaps beyond repair, by the simple flick of a whale tail.

Instead, those three orca whales gave me one of the most memorable experiences of my life, and the pictures to prove it. Sure, I was vulnerable, and I had no chance of escape. It was a close call of giant proportions. But what I *really* experienced was a felt sense of being touched by the whales and a feeling of being in tune with an ancient drive to survive. There was a momentary mutual regard between us, living beings on a journey, following some ancient route, somehow *together*. I felt blessed in that moment, connected to their power and grace, their agility and strength—and so, so grateful as our kayaks bobbed silently in the wake of their departure.

10

Looking Up

A picture-perfect fall day out on the playing field. Cool temps, blue sky. A soft breeze rustled through the tall, leafy cottonwood trees.

The flag football field formed the interior section of a city park that doubled as the outdoor playground and teaching area for my middle-school students.

"Okay, kids!" I shouted. "Let's divide up into teams! Take turns and say: 'peanut' or 'butter'!"

I didn't like this part. The process of making teams always seemed to leave someone out, so I had to make up ways to get even-numbered teams. Tall, short, male, female . . . Coed classes offered extra challenges if the numbers were off. My peanut butter routine was an attempt at randomization. My goal was to get the kids active and moving, making sure no one was left out. No one stood on the sidelines in my classes.

"Knock it off, Joey! No pushing! We have a game to get going!" As a middle school PE teacher I was always breaking up tangles and near fights. These kids had loads of energy but not much in the way of self-control.

"Miss Chase, can I be the quarterback?" asked Taylor a short kid with red, curly hair. I was sitting in my wheelchair, face-to-face with this wannabe quarterback. Teaching physical education from a wheelchair was all new for me in that eighth year of my career. It had only been five months since the accident that had paralyzed most of my lower body—and damaged my athletic identity. Now I was starting to get myself off the sidelines and back into the game by teaching out on that field again.

"Sure," I told him. "We'll take turns at all positions. You go first at quarterback." He smiled and turned toward the team, gripping the football a bit more confidently.

Teams divided; ball placed in center . . . I blew the whistle signaling it was time to start. The kids sprang into action.

I wanted a better view of the game, so I pushed myself up to standing with my forearm crutches. I'd only recently started walking again, using the crutches. I cheered the kids on, shouting instructions for legal flag-grabbing and ball-handling.

In the excitement, I stepped closer to the game.

A bit *too* close . . .

The rush of the ball handler, flag grabbers and cheering players moved down the sidelines ever closer to the goal. I, too, was caught up in the action—shouting, cheering, eyes glued to the game. The kid with the ball—the biggest one of the class of seventh-graders—ran down the sideline as opposing players reached for his flags. Like any good running back he was using the sideline in an effort to avoid the flag grabbers.

In a flash, I was hit. My crutches went flying, and suddenly I was lying flat on my back on the grass, staring up at the wide-eyed faces of middle-school students. The cheering had stopped.

"Miss Chase, are you okay?" several voices asked in unison. Their concern was obvious not just from their tone but from the looks on their faces.

From my new vantage point on the ground, my crutches lying next to me, I did a quick body scan for hurting places. None.

I checked my breathing—still working.

I checked my heart—still loving the kids, and teaching. I smiled and laughed out loud.

"Sure, kids!" I said. "I'm fine! And I'm so happy to be here on the ground, back in the game with you all!"

I meant it. No harm done. I was good. More than good. Great!

Five months in a rehab facility were done. I was happy to be back—even if I was lying on the ground. I was a teacher again, and these were my students. And what better way to let them know you can get knocked down—and that there's always a way to get back in the game?

Taylor pushed through the crowd, a look of real concern on his face.

"Miss Chase," he lamented. "I threw the pass, and he caught it and ran into you! I'm sorry!"

I smiled up at him. "It's okay. You made a great pass and he caught it! Would have been a touchdown if I didn't get in the way."

Using my best PE teacher voice, I shouted, "Go get my wheelchair, kids, I gotta get up! We have a game to finish!" I turned over, got up on my knees and, dragging my legs and feet along behind me, reached my wheelchair. I made one big thrust and a quick turn, and my bottom landed in the seat.

"Alright," I shouted, dusting the grass out of my hair—a little shaken, but steady. "Let's gets this game going!"

11

Backside of a Rock Face

I was with my middle-school students at Camp Red Cloud, a rugged outdoor education complex in the San Juan National Forest, which had a stunning backdrop of fourteen-thousand-foot mountains. The fall weather was kicking in, with bright, clear blue skies, a crisp morning breeze and aspens starting to turn gold.

I had hiked, climbed, and slept out in these hills many times before my accident, spending summers as an instructor for the Colorado Outward Bound School leading small groups of adolescents into the wilderness for two-week expeditions.

The location for the day's activity—a rappel down a steep wall of rock—was reached first by a brief hike along a smooth trail, and then by a short, *steep* hike up the backside of the rock wall. I sat at the bottom of that wall in my chair, looking up, longing to go with my students—yet knowing that this time I would have to watch from below.

But Tom, today's leader, had a different idea. I heard him call to me: "Let's get you up to that rappel site, Terry!"

I turned to look at him as he approached.

"You can do the rappel," he continued. "We'll lower you over the edge first so you can show the kids how it's done!"

Feeling uncertain, I said, "Sure . . . But how?"

Seriously: how could I climb that rock in a wheelchair? I was familiar with rock climbs and rappels from my pre-injury Outward Bound days, and I knew this would be an important experience for students. It wasn't just about learning the techniques involved, but also about facing the challenges of the climb. Climbing days often pushed these kids to the edges of their confidence and perceived limitations, teaching them powerful lessons about themselves that they could carry through life long after the course was completed.

My job had always been to facilitate the emotional and mental processes as students worked the physical challenges. Most often the internal limitations of doubt, worry and lack of self-confidence held them back or stalled their progress. Now it seemed I had to turn that process back around on myself and face my fears and limitations around being in a wheelchair.

"How do you plan on getting me up there?" I asked. Tom was a young man with powerful arm and back muscles. I could almost imagine him carrying me.

"We're gonna take the horse up there," he said, smiling. "You good with that?"

"Ah . . . sure," I said, a little quieter now, as new self-doubts and fears arose. The thought of getting on a horse was daunting. Even before my injury I hadn't had that much experience riding, and I certainly hadn't been on a horse since the accident.

On the other hand, I was not good at admitting hesitation or that I could not do something. I typically just didn't let anyone know I was afraid and went forward anyway.

"Sure," I said. "I can ride a horse. I rode some before I got hurt. Where's the horse?"

"Right here, Terry!" someone else shouted. I turned around to see an unsaddled, tall, white horse walking along the flat trail towards me, led by another young instructor. I looked up at the horse with awe and a little fear. He was beautiful! His name was Joe, and he was a handsome, well-muscled horse from Camp Red Cloud's stable of trail horses. Feeling small in my chair as this big horse came closer, I gripped the wheel rims tighter. My breath became shallow and short. He was magnificent in stature, head held high and eyes bright. He reminded me of the first horse I had taken care of when I was a teenager. I reached up and touched his soft, warm face and felt tears welling up inside me.

Joe was a good fit as my partner. He had that calm, unflappable look that horses (and people) wear when nothing seems to bothers them. I was still wondering, however, what the plan was—not just for mounting him, but also for the eventual proposed ride up that steep trail to the top.

"I'll get on Joe first," said Tom, "and then we'll get you up behind me. You can hold on to me as we go up the backside of the hill." He either didn't notice or pretended *not* to notice the look of surprise on my face.

I hesitated slightly, but not long enough to let anyone think I was afraid. "Okay . . . If you guys think this'll work."

They walked Joe closer to my wheelchair—and he did not seem to mind. Tom mounted him first and held him at a standstill. Two other instructors stationed themselves on either side of me, ready to assist. I pushed up to stand with their help, reaching to the back of the horse. I stood straight, stiff, and as tall as my legs would allow. The two helpers leaned over, grabbed my lower legs, and with a quick "1-2-3," up I went onto the back of the horse.

I wrapped my arms tight around Tom's waist. My half-paralyzed legs dangled on either side of Joe's back.

"Hold on, Terry," Tom said. "I don't want you sliding off Joe as we go." He laughed at his little joke and rhyme.

Joe kept his head down as he lifted his hooves up and over and around the small rocks, bushes, and loose dirt on the trail. The short ride uphill evoked memories from a long time ago: walking these mountains with a heavy pack, leading students to high rock climbs.

At the top we were greeted with a wide view of the surrounding forest and high mountain peaks. The air was clear and crisp.

Joe had carried me to a place I would never have been able to get to in that wheelchair.

Dismounting was easier than mounting. The two helpers were ready to receive me as I slowly slid off to the side of Joe. No wheelchair this time. I landed on a cushion to protect my bony hind end and scooted away from the horse. I thanked everyone who had gotten me up there, but especially Joe. I had trusted him, and he had trusted me. And thanks to him I was back where I belonged.

I turned around and saw my students waiting for me at the top of that rock face, their faces in a state of awe that I had been delivered by horse to this unique classroom setting. Always the teacher, I started the lesson of the morning. It was time to suit up with a harness, ropes and instructions on the rappelling activity. I had a partner who would be my safety, assuring that the ropes would be handled properly and allowing gravity to take me down the rock face. We practiced our specific communication commands—for example, "on belay" meaning I was roped on and he was too. I scooted to the edge of the rock face, turned over on my belly, let my legs dangle over and carefully pushed off while my partner held me steady. At this edge, I was teaching myself and the kids, that life will always be a choice of stepping across edges, unknown and scary. Yet with trusting, awareness and good support, we can do a lot more than we think.

12

Edge of Dark

March, 1989. I sat in the warm sun at the edge of the high canyon wall overlooking the Green River. Except for a few noisy hawks, the desert was quiet. Warm winds swirled up from the canyon floor hundreds of feet below, stirring the sand around me.

The spot had a particularly clear and open view, and it was the perfect place to wait for Al to catch up and join me at day's end of our three-day camping excursion. My teaching partner and I were exploring the rugged White Rim Trail in Canyonlands National Park, in southeast Utah. The 110-mile trail runs through a remote, desolate wilderness and is for dedicated hikers, mountain bikers and off-road enthusiasts, especially for those who love the desert.

I had driven a few miles ahead of Al in my four-wheel drive truck. I was driving the support and gear vehicle on this trip; Al was riding his mountain bike. Over the course of the last three days we'd split up in the morning, each going at our separate paces, and then meeting again in late afternoon at our assigned campsite, where we'd share stories of the day's adventures. I'd tell Al of my scary drives over rocks, soft, sandy roads and narrow passageways, often with precipitous cliff edges only a few feet away from me. He'd tell stories of his cycling adventures over the same roads, which were often too steep and rocky for even the most skillful and powerful riders.

Now I waited for him, sitting in my wheelchair contemplating the vastness before me and considering rolling myself over the edge, off the Canyonlands ledge and into the open air. That empty space was calling to me. The idea of shedding the confinement of my wheelchair was appealing. I wanted to feel the cool, clear air of the canyons rush past me and be free of the metal rolling machine I was trapped in.

It wasn't that I consciously wanted to kill myself, which of course would have been the result of my impulse in the moment. *I just wanted out of that wheelchair.*

***

The thought of ending it all had crossed my mind many times since the accident a year before.

If not for the accident and that wheelchair I would have been biking the strenuous mountain trail, struggling alongside my long-time friend. But I could no longer hike trails or ride bikes off-road. I'd lost my ability to explore and be free in the wilderness, to walk miles through the mountain valleys of Colorado and the desert canyons of southern Utah. I could not heave the weight of a fully loaded pack onto my back and walk away from the city into the open lands. I could not even take a long bike ride after a day of teaching middle-school kids.

It wasn't simply the physical freedom that I missed; it was the emotional release and exhilaration as well. I was used to handling the stressors of teaching and daily life through physical outlets like hiking and biking. These activities calmed me. I had found solace in the natural world, which to me was a spiritual place of worship; I could center myself in the midst of its beauty.

Now my world had different struggles, and I couldn't escape them on my bike. Many times, after my injury I'd go into very dark places within myself. For a long time, I couldn't bring myself to share with anyone the pain and struggle of having been a very active young woman who now needed a wheelchair to get around.

Sometimes simply being out in public was too much to handle. People would avert their eyes when I rolled past, or someone would stare at me as I pulled into a handicapped parking place, as if I didn't belong there either. At times like those I would feel myself collapse inward. I'd want to hide, to disappear. I'd want to just *end it*. Put myself out of my misery and be done.

But something always drew me back from the edge of that darkness.

***

Three years after the injury I was poised on a different edge— that of a cold, metal exam table in the sterile, bland office of a general medicine physician. My legs dangled off the table, swinging freely, though not fully functional.

I was waiting for the physician to enter. This appointment would help determine the extent of my disability so that I could receive disability retirement from the school district. I had decided to leave my beloved role as a middle-school PE teacher and change careers to something else—as yet unknown.

One of my goals after the accident had been to return to teaching, and in the days, months and years after my accident, I displayed abilities as a physical educator and coach that far exceeded my expectations. At the same time, I never fully met my own high standards of what it meant to be a good teacher. So eventually I decided it was time to move on.

That day on the exam table I put my weakness, my paralysis, and my physical losses on full display. It was crucial for the doctor to thoroughly evaluate my state of functioning in order to determine whether I was eligible for disability retirement.

A young, clean-shaven, professional-looking doctor entered the room, head bowed over a medical chart, barely glancing at me.

"Hello, Miss Chase," he said, eyes still glued to the file he was holding. "Today I'm going to do an examination to determine your level of function with this spinal cord injury."

I didn't like hearing that, even though I knew that was exactly what he had to do. For three years now I had approached this paralysis as a challenge to rise above. In my mind, going forward, *nothing* would be impossible.

And yet here I was, required to *prove* that certain things were now, in fact, beyond my ability. It was confusing and demoralizing, even though I knew it had to be done this way for my retirement designation.

The doctor worked me over with the tools of his trade. He listened to my heart and lungs with his stethoscope. His otoscope peered into my ears and eyes, and he poked at my legs with sharp, metal objects and watched for signs of sensation. When he tapped his rubber-tipped hammer below my kneecaps to test my reflexes, my legs jumped in response to the tapping; this was a "hyper-reflex" reaction indicating loss of voluntary control.

I tried to hold back my feelings of anger and humiliation.

Still looking at his chart instead of directly at me, the doctor asked, "So, Miss Chase, what kinds of functional activities do you do in a day?"

He wanted to know if I could perform the usual activities of daily living: dressing, bathing, grooming, eating, and toileting. I wanted to tell him, "Of course I can take care of myself, you idiot. That's why I went to rehab—to be fully independent, to be a productive person again, to live in my house by myself and take my dog for walk."

But I answered politely, "I can do all activities of daily living on my own. I even get up and go to work every day." Just in case he thought that was important to know.

I didn't know what he thought. He just kept asking questions, barely acknowledging me or my answers. How independent was I? Did I live alone? Did I have assistance in my home? Mundane questions, which I answered in a mundane sort of way while my anger rose up and was swallowed back down again.

I wanted him to ask me things like:

"Are you able to go outdoors again?"

"How are you keeping yourself healthy and in shape?"

These were things I was proud of. They showed that I was capable. Instead a voice in my head kept saying, "He's more interested in my disability, not in me as a person."

And he was. That was his job that day.

This didn't change the fact that I hated not being seen as a person, but as a disabled patient.

The doctor got what he needed to complete the paperwork. The exam ended. I rolled myself out of the office, disgusted with the entire experience, feeling demeaned and dismissed as I climbed into my car and prepared to drive back to work, to my role as a productive citizen.

It didn't matter that I'd gone to the doctor precisely to receive an evaluation of "disabled." The experience had triggered and enraged me because it again laid bare the facts of the devastating changes in my physical being—and the related judgments I held against myself because of them.

If I'd had a gun in my hand, I would have shot myself that day in the parking garage. My irrational rage at the doctor for pointing out how disabled I really was . . . my humiliation at having him touch my cold, paralyzed legs . . . my self-disgust at being less than normal . . . All overwhelmed me.

Less than normal.

On the exam table that day the full realization had hit me harder than ever. I was no longer able to do my normal walking, hiking, biking, climbing. I couldn't play in the same way with my school kids, couldn't be a weekend soccer player or officiate basketball games. It had been three years since the accident, and still the anger and grief raged inside me like ocean waves crashing against a rocky shore.

***

Sometimes the dark edge spoke to my hand as it held the steering wheel while I drove down the highway. Maybe the voice was triggered by a sudden feeling of inadequacy, or remembering something someone had said to me, or a certain look I'd received that tapped the well of anger within me. I would feel my right-hand start clenching, and I'd want to jerk the steering wheel of the SUV off the road. I sometimes had to pull that hand off the wheel and hold it in my lap or tuck it under my thigh to keep myself from flipping the vehicle at sixty-five miles an hour. The rage nearly overtook any rational thoughts about how destructive highway suicide was—not just for me, but for anyone else on the road with me.

***

I was at the edge of that dark place many times over the years following my injury. Yet even though there were times I wanted to roll myself over a cliff, shoot myself or flip my car while speeding down the highway, I obviously never followed through. I also tried to run away from the hurt, resentment and fears, to just block it all out, but that didn't work either.

Then I discovered what I had to do.

I had to admit to myself that I was human after all.

I had to go *into* the dark place and see what was there.

I had to face the darkness.

And step into the light.

And in doing so I discovered I had the power to keep going.

***

Gradually, I learned to live again.

I learned to get back outdoors, to use specialized equipment made for people with disabilities. Bicycling became hand cycling, and I rode many, many miles using just upper body muscle. My competitive spirit was engaged when I learned wheelchair tennis. I paddled into the wilderness in a sea kayak. I took up swimming, dog walking, horseback riding, waterskiing and cross-country skiing. Slowly my fear and anger and frustration were overtaken by renewed sensations of discovery and joy.

My search for new challenges also took me on journeys of self-forgiveness and healing, so that I discovered a power within myself that no one else could give me. I was grateful for a trusted therapist, Janet, and my partner, Sharon, but in truth nothing outside of me could by itself heal the pain and scars, or take away the dysfunction. I travelled through those valleys of grief, through the anger and hurt, which meant facing and mourning my losses. In allowing others to love me just as I was, I had to learn to give up control. I claimed access to my inner worlds of spirituality, consciousness and caring. I realized that I have much to give back to the world, especially to those who are hurting and mourning their own losses.

What I *didn't* do was run away. I didn't go through with any of the "escape plans" that would have plunged me irrevocably into the darkness. I found a way out, over and through.

I said above that I learned to live again. But it might be truer to say that I learned, maybe for the first time in my life, to *truly* live. I stepped back from the edge of the dark and into the light of living. I learned to feel more in a body that had lost feeling and function than I'd ever felt before that body was broken.

The edge of the dark was always there—as it may be for most of us—but I eventually learned to let the light in.

Spoke 2

13

Flinging Forward

How can a person in a wheelchair get accepted into—much less complete—nursing school?

I didn't even ask myself that when I first considered applying for the Nursing Doctorate degree at the University of Colorado. Instead, I simply followed my impulse, inspired initially by a brief newspaper article about the program—which was based on the Theory of Human Caring and taught by nursing theorist Jean Watson, Ph.D., RN, and other high-level faculty members. The program included not only formal training in nursing but also incorporated aspects of the arts and a holistic approach to health care. I was stirred and intrigued, and a familiar, quiet voice within urged me to apply. That voice didn't say anything about whether my being in a wheelchair would get in the way.

So, wisdom, hunch—whatever it was—I decided to follow what amounted to a calling from deep inside myself.

As I learned more about the program, I began to have the usual doubts about myself and my own capabilities. The doctoral program would take four years to complete. It was full-time and year-round, with undergraduate nursing classes, upper-level preparation and four thousand hours of hands-on clinical work in all aspects of nursing. These challenges did not stop me from applying—I decided I would just "figure it out" when I got there, and so flung myself forward.

My credentials were good. I had returned to teaching only five months after my accident. I had ten years' experience as an educator. I had earned a Master's Degree in Exercise Physiology in 1990, just two years after being paralyzed. Now, two years later, it felt like the right time to pursue a Doctorate in Nursing (ND) in a field that would allow me to continue my quest to understand what had helped me feel better after the accident— which would in turn help me serve others the way I had been served on my path to recovery.

I wrote the required application essays based on my experience as a patient, but I struggled with filling in the blank on the "I want to be a nurse because—" section. Why? Because I had little desire to become "just" a bedside nurse. I saw myself in the role of teacher and figured I would *teach* nursing more than practice it like a "typical" bedside nurse did.

I had not yet put two and two together to realize that those "typical" bedside nurses were the very same ones who had helped me through my toughest times.

I had much to learn.

I submitted the application and was promptly rejected. This landed hard. Sure, *I* had doubts about myself, but I never imagined they would not want me in the program. Obviously I got that wrong. At the same time, the rejection drove home to me that I *really* wanted to be part of this program. My determination came from deep within.

Regarding my rejection, I had to ask: was it because of my injury and being in a wheelchair? Surely they couldn't assess that without talking with me about it? *I* knew the wheelchair would not be a barrier.

These and other thoughts ran through my head in the days following my rejection, but they all boiled down to one thing: I had to reapply. So, within a week I had an appointment with the program director to discuss my application and see what had gone wrong.

The director was kind and welcoming. The wall behind her desk was decorated with numerous degrees and plaques that spoke to a distinguished nursing career. After she thanked me for coming in, I asked her simply, "I would really like to know why I wasn't accepted into the program. Is it my injury and the fact that I use a wheelchair?"

She had my application on her desk and kept her eyes on it as she flipped through the pages. "I've been looking at your application and notes from the admissions committee," she said. "I see they had a concern about your ability to perform CPR on a patient. Basically, we need to know if you can handle the duties of being a nurse at the bedside, whether you're physically capable of the basic requirements."

I felt my defensiveness rise and replied with restraint. "I really don't think that will be a problem for me. I know how to get myself safely onto the floor and perform the needed lifesaving measures. In fact, I've practiced and performed adequately for CPR certification and advanced cardiac life support." Inside, I was pleading: *Just give me a chance to prove that I can do this! I am capable! I am sure about this! Believe in me!*

This was one of those times I really hated being in my wheelchair.

"I want to help people," I said. "I've been a patient with spinal cord injury. I want to know the ins and outs of what helped me feel better through an unbelievably bad time in my life. I know it had a lot to do with the nurses and other providers in my acute care and rehab hospital. And I'm intrigued by the theory of human caring, too."

I slowed myself down, trying to show the right balance of thoughtfulness and passion. "I'm curious—is that what helped me so much? The caring part? I had medicines and treatments and lots of physical therapy, but I'm not sure that those are the only things that made me well. So I want to learn more about human caring in the nursing environment, and I believe this program will help me do that."

She was looking directly at me now, and I could see both fatigue and caring in her eyes. She nodded for me to continue, and I did.

"I know it might seem weird that I'm trying to get into nursing school. I'm not oblivious to the hard work of nursing: the physical labor, long hours, and emotional circumstances needing attention in a shift. But being in this wheelchair has made me exceptionally good at problem-solving. I'm aware of the safety issues and how the patient will always come first. And I'm willing to ask for help and to assure everyone around me that I'm aware of the risks. I guess all I'm really asking for is a chance to prove that I can do this. My wheelchair may be perceived by others as a problem, but it is not a problem for me, and I believe I can demonstrate this."

This was and is a familiar refrain in my life: the wheelchair will not limit me. I am determined to use it to my advantage and not be a victim of circumstance.

I knew from my experience as a patient that the profession of nursing is not easy. I experienced the unseen and underappreciated aspects of nursing. During my long nights after the accident, doubts, anger and sadness blended seamlessly with sleeplessness and grief. At those times, night shift nurses stood at my bedside to simply be with me. I vividly remember how they helped me feel better, and how they listened to and supported me as I struggled through those hard nights.

They acknowledged my pain and doubt without judgment, only acceptance. That was the kind of nurse I wanted to be. That was what fueled my desire to move forward, no matter the difficulty.

I did my best expressing all this to the program director, and something must have hit home. My second—thoroughly revised and improved—application was accepted.

***

In 1992 the University of Colorado School of Nursing building was one of the oldest in Denver's busy medical complex. It had been retrofitted with a steep concrete ramp to the front door and one small elevator. It did not have any automatic door openers, and restrooms were only marginally accessible. I would become quite familiar with these and other quirky ADA modifications during the next four years.

Nervous, excited, and scared to death: that describes me at the start of that program, ready to embark on a whole new chapter of my life as one of the thirteen students in that year's cohort. I was the only student using a wheelchair.

I met my fellow classmates in a large, open conference room on the first day school. The ND program required previous college degrees, so my new classmates were educated in various fields. Many had work experience outside of healthcare. Joan was a teacher, Pam a drug and alcohol counselor, Ted an environmental engineer. A few had small families and children to care for. Some were single or, like me, living with a significant other. We would become close friends over the next four years.

Introductory orientation included meeting core faculty members, getting a class schedule for the semester, and basically seeing in black and white an outline for the next four years of my life. Classes and clinical placements were detailed for us, and a long list of required books was handed out. It was all very exciting, and daunting as well. How often do you know in advance, and in such detail, what the next four years of life will hold? And yet, even with all this preparation, the next four years were unpredictable and full of surprises.

The Nursing Doctorate program was very new and innovative in the crowded and often confusing field of nursing education, with varying levels of education and one standard exam to become a registered nurse (RN). This degree would be one more added to the field of nursing education options. As the third cohort of ND students, we soon learned that the program directors and faculty were still working out many details. This made for an uneasy start to a rigorous program, but it also had the incidental benefit of teaching us early on that nurses must be flexible, nimble, and able to engage with the unexpected. It was an intense program too: four full years of classroom learning and four thousand hours of clinical practice in all areas of healthcare. The final year consisted of a full-time hospital residency. Once we got started there was not much time for anything else.

14

Hard Lessons

The first week consisted of classes and practice sessions in the school's mock hospital unit, beginning with the foundations of nursing: making a bed, giving a mock bed bath to a fellow student (who played the role of patient), placing and removing bedpans without spilling the contents, and so on. I quickly found myself frustrated by the emphasis on these basic skills—which seemed to highlight my inadequacies. I wanted to get on to that higher level of nursing care that had attracted me to the program in the first place.

One day in class I expressed this out loud. "I thought this was a program on human caring—how to meet the patient as a human being and break down barriers to quality care."

The clinical faculty member instructing the class was kind but firm in her reprimand. "Ms. Chase, I hear your frustrations. I also want to remind you that the foundations of nursing care include the safe handling of patients. The tools you're learning now and the ability to take care of a patient's basic physical needs are vital to human caring. If we can't handle the basic needs of the people in our care, they will not be ready for anything else."

Enough said. I was officially schooled.

This was a lesson I needed to learn. I had been approaching the idea of nursing from the lofty plane of seeing caring as a mental construct, with some positive emotional support thrown in for good measure. I needed to learn—early on—that nursing *is* that, but it's also down-and-dirty: roll up your sleeves, heave-ho, make the bed, empty the bedpan, and do whatever else needs to be done. All those things, however mundane and dirty, connect a nurse to the human experience of the patient.

With that newfound realization, I got down and dirty learning the skills required in my clinical assignments. I made those beds, placed and emptied those bed pans, washed the face of a stiff mannequin patient. I learned to maneuver my wheelchair around the small hospital-room space.

Little did I know, I was in denial about how much I had suffered during my own hospital stay. My experience as a nurse would help me come to terms with what I'd experienced as a patient. This was an unexpected side effect of the program.

15

Finding My Voice

"Okay," Professor Janson announced to the class. "Let's have everyone pair up. One person get in the bed as the patient. The other one plays the nurse and practices the range-of-motion activities we reviewed earlier."

I knew what "range of motion" exercises were. I'd had them done to me every day of my rehab patient experience. These stretching exercises are designed to keep the muscles and joints supple and flexible. Because of my paralysis I was unable to do these on my own, so a therapist would have to lift and stretch and push my legs to their limit. Without normal movement, my body would eventually stiffen up and become contracted, decreasing my mobility. I became used to having other people move my body parts around when I was not able to do myself. I knew they wouldn't be a problem for me to perform on a patient—except for the fact that I was sitting in a wheelchair and my student partner was up on a hospital bed.

"Alright," I said to Jeff, "let's figure this out."

Jeff was a tall, lanky guy lying comfortably in the middle of the bed.

"Jeff, I know you're being a good patient right now, but I'm gonna need some help to perform this range of motion exercise safely and effectively."

"Oh sure, Terry. I forgot you were in a wheelchair." I took his passing comment as a major, if unintended, compliment. "What do you have in mind?"

"If we lower the bed down some, I can reach your legs and do the range of motion, at least partway. I don't want to make a big deal out of this. I don't want any special treatment, and I don't think it's cheating to lower the bed."

I looked around for Professor Janson to ask her, but she was occupied observing another group of students. I knew she'd get to us eventually. I adjusted the hospital bed to a height even with my knees, then reached for Jeff's left leg and lifted it high, holding it with steady pressure and not too much pull. My arms and shoulders worked at maximum effort to lift and stretch the hamstrings of his leg.

"Can you feel that stretch in your hamstrings as I lift?" I asked, with strain in my voice. "Am I getting some range of motion going for you?" Jeff was a healthy guy, athletic and with firm muscles. I wanted to get enough leverage to make the stretch happen.

"Yes," he said. "You're doing good. Now how about my other leg? I can scoot a little closer to the edge if you think that will help."

"Sure, let's try it." I was game for any kind of work-around, within reason. It was a time of extreme problem-solving—not only was I trying to master the basic skill, but also to learn how to do it properly in a wheelchair.

Professor Janson's voice rose up behind me. "Miss Chase, may I see you do that left-leg range of motion one more time? I was busy with another student and didn't observe it."

Here we go again, I said to myself. I was sure she expected me to fail, or at least to do something that wasn't up to required standards. I had the feeling that despite what she said she'd been watching me even when she was with other groups of students.

"Sure," I said. "Jeff and I figured this out, and it worked well for me. I'm happy to do it again. Jeff, are you ready?"

I demonstrated the moves again . . . and again. And again. Each time I did the prescribed range of motion exercise, Professor Janson found something that needed correction or fine-tuning. It seemed to me that I had never heard that much detailed feedback given to any other student.

By the time the session was winding down I was sweating and angry. I had reached a boiling point. My feelings of hating the wheelchair and being unable to perform in the same fashion as my classmates were all-consuming. And of course, it was made worse by what I perceived to be constant scrutiny and correction.

As the class period came to an end, I spoke up. "Excuse me, Professor Janson, may I have a moment after class? I have a question for you."

She looked a little startled. "Of course," she said. "Let me close up the room, and we can sit in the corridor and talk."

As she fussed around the room, throwing sheets back on the beds, I formulated what I would say. I was fuming inside with a mixture of anger, disgust, and inadequacy. At the same time, I knew that blowing up in frustration wouldn't be effective or even remotely professional.

Professor Janson, looking fatigued, sat down in a lounge chair and seemed curious as to what I would bring up.

I said, "Thanks for talking with me. I'm feeling very scrutinized. It feels like it's above and beyond what the rest of my cohort is getting for feedback. It's like you're waiting for me to fail or do something unsafe." Again I found myself working to keep my frustration in check. "I want you to know that I'm careful, and I'm always aware of the safety of the patient. Like, today, I worked with Jeff to figure out a solution that I think stayed within a normal range of adjustments. And I will ask for help when needed. I just . . . feel the heat of so much scrutiny. Is it possible to take that spotlight off me when we're practicing these skills?"

Her eyes conveyed worry and even some sorrow. She said slowly, "Terry, I'm concerned you'll get hurt in that wheelchair. The positions are so unnatural, and you could strain a muscle or hurt a tendon. In all my twenty-five years of nursing in hospitals and academia, I've never seen a nurse in a wheelchair." She looked at the floor as she spoke, perhaps not sure how I might take her remarks.

"Professor, I can assure you that my being in a wheelchair will not be a barrier for me, and that it won't negatively affect my care for patients. I am a minority in the profession—I get that—but nurses have always been problem-solvers. I am taking that to another level. Safety is at the forefront for me and my patients at all times."

"Okay, then," she said, lifting her sad, heavy eyes. "I appreciate your willingness and your perseverance. I trust you will ask for my help in problem-solving these skills as we practice. I know you're keeping the safety of the patient and yourself at the highest level. I will certainly take that spotlight off. Okay?"

"Sure," I said. "Thank you for listening and hearing me out." I felt relieved and grateful in that moment. I knew this would not be the last time I had to have to have this conversation with an instructor or preceptor, when I had to stand up for myself and defend my commitment to nursing. The barriers, both architectural and attitudinal, were revealing themselves even before I was in an actual clinical setting. And those barriers rose up on both the outside—via my teachers, mentors and supervisors in the program—and on the inside, from my own insecurities.

16

Be Bigger than My Chair

The semesters and years wore on. Classes increased in intensity and demand. I was constantly hauling around multiple heavy books in a bag on my lap. My weekends and holidays were spent in the university library and I had much less personal time with Sharon. Exercise consisted solely of pushing my wheelchair up the steep, concrete ramp leading into the School of Nursing (at least I got to speed down it at the end of the day) and across campus. Over the four years I spent in school I replaced several sets of tires thanks to the beating they took on the urban campus.

Slowly I developed a new persona: *be bigger than my chair.*

Whenever I rolled into a new clinical setting or assignment in the community, I rose up inside and met whomever I needed to meet full-on, my eyes looking straight into theirs and my energy confident and secure. I made sure they saw me first—not the wheelchair.

This took place gradually, but I had ample opportunity for practice: multiple clinical placements in the community, various hospital units and even a locked adolescent psychiatric ward. It took a lot of energy to always be bigger than I was feeling. I had to be ready to prove myself beyond the shadow of a doubt. So even if a task was mundane, I performed above and beyond. There were many times over the years of classwork, clinicals and nursing preceptors where proving myself was exhausting and I considered leaving and going into something simpler. Icing donuts frequently crossed my mind as much easier than following my calling into the nursing profession.

17

Foundations of Caring

I persevered. And it helped that there were many faculty members who saved me in those times of doubt.

Janet Quinn, Ph.D., RN, seemed to float into our classrooms. Her kindness and gentle spirit moved me to tears many a time. She taught the importance of presence in the moment just by her beingness. In her classes there were no long lectures, just discussions held in a circle, many times without even a textbook. Janet taught therapeutic touch and the ways in which energy work could be incorporated into nursing practice. Our first assignment was to write and then share our autobiography. This brought us all together, with tears flowing as we heard each other's stories of struggles and triumphs. This helped us to see each other as fellow human beings and evoked a powerful reminder of the shared humanity of provider and patient.

Jean Watson, Ph.D., RN, nursing theorist, and Dean of the School of Nursing shared her vision for a more holistic and caring nursing practice. Her flamboyant style of dress and her artistic talent helped me know that healing could be supported through art, music, literature and creativity. I learned more about the Theory of Human Caring, which was what had initially inspired me to pursue nursing. She also introduced us to chaos theory as it related to the human system, and to an appreciation for the order that appeared in the chaos if we looked for it.

And I learned a *lot*. Physiology, microbiology, pharmacology, and nursing informatics were core to our becoming skilled and knowledgeable nurses. Kathy McGivley, Ph.D., RN, hired me as a research assistant for her project looking at health care systems for elders living in rural areas of the state. My job—organizing and categorizing hundreds of photos—could be done at any hour of the day or night, and Kathy trusted me to get it done. I was able to make some extra money while learning even more about the field of nursing through the eyes of a renowned researcher.

There was no question from any of these faculty members as to my capabilities as a nurse—or as a human being. There was simply guidance and unconditional acceptance.

My clinical experiences offered a strong foundation in all areas of nursing: mother-baby to adolescent healthcare, geriatric care, mental health, community health with the migrant populations, operating room, and emergency department. I was trained well to be a skilled generalist nurse. At one point I even returned to the western slope of Colorado in Grand Junction—a three-week night shift rotation in the acute care hospital where I had been cared for after my critical injury only five years before.

In this nursing program we were challenged to expand the possibilities of a caring profession. Countless hours were spent reading and integrating research to be translated into actual practice. As I worked through these four intense and rewarding years, I became aware that I was not the only student struggling with self-esteem and confidence. I gradually realized that the spotlight that seemed to be shining on me all the time was actually powered in part by my own self-judgments and high expectations.

When I rolled across the stage with my cohort of fellow students—thirteen graduates of the Nursing Doctorate program—at the end of that four years, I was transformed. I was ready to use the twin superpowers of caring and clinical skills.

I heard—and followed—my call.

I became a nurse in a wheelchair.

Little did I know this was only the first step in creating my career as healthcare provider, a nurse with so much to give, so much to offer and so much desire to help others as I had been helped in my own healing process.

18

Windchime

Eight years past the accident.

I was still struggling with letting go of my able-bodied picture of myself. The strong legs and back that powered me up and over mountain passes and rock walls; bike rides of forty-plus miles; long days on the field with kids playing sports . . . I was stuck between the worlds of able-bodied and dis-able-bodied.

As if I needed additional evidence that something bad had happened, I still carried with me the crumpled frame of the bicycle I'd been riding at the time of the accident. A mass of twisted metal with gears and cables dangling from it. I'd been carrying it with me for years, as if it were a precious book or article of clothing.

Why? I think as a reminder of the life I'd had pre-accident. If it had been the size of a pendant I'd have hung it around my neck. But the bike was an ungainly mess: dusty, dirty, no longer in ridable shape, and with a fading tag hanging off it:

Evidence Tag
Case # 88-08757
Officer: D. Oswalt #359
Date/Time: 04-02-88 1600
Items: D1
Location: ~700 block S. 5th Street

But it was *my bike*—and *my life*. I could not just throw it away like a piece of trash. I could not simply let it go. Just as I could not let go of the image of myself as a strong, athletic, walking, running, hiking, biking, jumping, climbing and upright woman. I was eight years into this sudden change—which really was no longer "sudden" but instead a constant daily condition. Sure, I was independent in daily activities: driving a vehicle, holding a job and now entering the nursing profession. But there was still something holding me back from going forward and adjusting to this life change. I could not let go of that mangled bike and all it represented to me. Nor could I let go of my longing to return to my life "before."

And then I shared with a good friend that I was still carrying around my mangled mess of a bike, and she had an idea.

"Terry let's turn that bike into something else," she said. "I don't know exactly what, but I've got lots of tools, and you know I love a creative art project."

Peggy was an occupational therapist on the adolescent psychiatric unit at Children's Hospital. At that time I was there for one of my three-week nursing rotations, learning how older children and adolescents struggling with mental and emotional challenges received inpatient psychiatric care and treatment. Peggy helped the kids with adjustments in their thinking using creative arts and facilitated conversations. She was easy to talk to, and I found myself sharing more about my own mental and emotional struggles with her, which is what led to the current discussion.

"Are you suggesting we transform it into something altogether different?" I replied, both curious and skeptical. Something about the idea moved me; I felt a stir of possibility. That frame meant so much to me, but it also felt like I was holding onto something old and no longer useful.

"Yes! You know, maybe a windchime or something? Creative arts is a great way to make the invisible visible. Maybe this process will help you move on? I love my bikes too. I get how difficult it is for you to let that thing go. What do you say? I've got Thursday evening open. I'll bring my tools."

I saw that moment for what it was: an invitation to step forward. To let go of something old and grab onto something new in the same moment.

"Okay," I said. "Let's do this."

And so the transformative process was set in motion.

Peggy brought her metal cutting tools, a blow torch and her gift of artistry. I brought my dusty, mangled bike frame and we set up shop on the back porch.

"Let's just saw the top and down tubes into lengths of about ten inches," Peggy said, referring to the top bar of the frame and the one that angled down from the front of the bike. "I think they can be the wind chime tubes."

"Okay," I said, with some hesitation. I still didn't have much of an idea of what we were doing. I had seen wind chimes before and of course had a basic idea, but we didn't have a blueprint or specific design in mind. I really just had to trust Peggy.

As the sparks from the metal saw went flying, my emotions were all over the place. I was scared and sad about my bike frame being sawed apart. I was excited to see something new come from it. There was a sense of not knowing what to expect or what the product would look like. I was challenged to trust and go with the flow.

I was not particularly good at that part.

I had always had a plan, a design to follow.

This time, however, that familiar pattern was not working. I had to trust like never before.

As Peggy wielded the heavy cutting equipment, I worked on disentangling the brake cables, and taking apart the chain rings. Eventually the different pieces of what had been a tangled mess of metal and wire were laid out side by side. We began to fashion a windchime.

It took several hours that spring evening. Sawing and hammering and re-fitting pieces of dangling cables and metal and nuts and bolts into a windchime.

The bottom bracket of the bike became the suspension platform. Five strings of wire were passed through this bracket, and the larger and smaller chain rings helped form the shape. Each of the tubes from the bike frame were hung so that they touched the chain rings; when they moved in the wind they'd strike the ring and make a sound. The various chain rings hung in descending size. We used brake cables for hanging and to string together the tubes. Finally, the back reflector was hung to catch the wind like a sail and set the various parts of the chime in motion.

It was dark when we finished, and I was still not sure it would work—up until the moment we hung the piece on the hook of the covered back porch and listened to it sing a new tune in the evening breeze. I was tired, hungry . . . and yet so happy with the creation of the windchime, this reclaiming of my bike in a new form.

That windchime became a symbol of change, of transformation. It helped me know that I too could transform into something new. I could begin to let go of the images of myself pre-injury, and create myself anew.

The windchime brought a sense of possibility. I didn't know what my future would look like, but I could hold a vision for what it *could* be. I knew that I wanted to use my injury to move forward. I would not let it hold me back.

I would use it to transform myself, to catch the wind and make new music in the world.

19

Step into the Light

I didn't walk this journey of discovery and transformation alone.

In addition to the many angels I've described thus far, I found a therapist named Janet. She helped me process my anger on all the various levels I experienced it. She provided a loving, caring platform of acceptance from which I could handle my anger without destroying myself. I learned to be in contact with emotions that had been stuffed and stuck down for so long.

Janet helped me when I was in those dark, dark places. She laughed and cried with me. Once we even went for a chocolate ice cream soda to celebrate some success in my therapy.

For over ten years, including the time I was in the nursing doctoral program, Janet was my counselor, mentor, and friend. With her guidance and skill, I worked through many traumatic issues, even those beyond the accident and back into my early childhood and adolescence—issues that had kept me stuck and angry. She kept working with me through the years as I would make progress and then retreat to old familiar patterns. I was getting that remaining stuck in those patterns was not helpful to my moving forward and having a life of freedom. Janet loved me through it all, the dark times and the times of lightness and happiness.

It was during these times that she was diagnosed and struggled with breast cancer. The treatments and surgeries never daunted her commitment to me or her other clients; she never wavered in her support.

Her gentle yet powerful style of working with me was something I wanted to learn. Janet never pushed or even suggested I consider the same Master's degree that she held: Spiritual Psychology, from the University of Santa Monica. I simply took it in through my work with her, both on the practical side of how she ran her practice, but also through the powerful transformational processes as they unfolded within me.

At some point the thought of attending the Spiritual Psychology program at USM came to me naturally. The realization that this would be the next step in the progression of my journey to find out what helped me feel better about my injury and my life.

What attracted to me to this program? The emphasis on spirituality. My educational progression took me through physical, mental and emotional learning processes. I knew the spiritual realm would be the next level of learning for me. The USM program offered a transformational soul-level of healing, which to me meant deeper growth and an expanded sense of internal freedom. I wanted to develop these things within myself, and then help others do the same.

It would not be an easy path.

The two-year program was one weekend a month for nine

months each year, with an additional week in the summers. In addition to tuition I'd have to pay for travel, lodging and food.

Sharon gave me her support while cautioning me about the immense commitment—which was brave of her, because my previous graduate program ground me to dust and strained our relationship.

I set positive intentions for this to work in my favor. I made a vision board for attracting all available support into my life. I asked for assistance from my employer for tuition reimbursement. I knew a friend in the airlines who could offer me free flights. I configured my work weeks to be off on Fridays so I could catch the late morning flight and arrive just in time for the Friday evening class. The weekend class schedule was full: Friday evenings, and all day Saturday and Sunday until late afternoon. I'd take the earliest flight out of LAX on Monday morning, at 6:00 a.m. and be back in Denver to arrive at work by 9:30 a.m.

And I ate light to save money.

I knew from the first weekends that this would be like no other educational experience of my life. The first basic skill we learned—Seeing the Loving Essence—was the key to my own healing. I had spent so much of life disliking myself and keeping my true loving, laughing self hidden, but this soon started to change.

I will not detail the entire experience here—just share a few aspects of the process—because there is no easy or short way to express it. The coursework was experiential; very little lecturing, arguing or debating. We just got down to the business of learning and practicing numerous of basic skills infused with a loving, spiritual sense, counseling techniques and psychology modalities. There were intense assignments between weekend classes involving writing, journaling, and exploring deep questions.

I began to notice myself being kinder and more open to others, and not as judgmental or reactive when things did not go my way. I learned to apply loving to the parts of myself that hurt. One activity was a "relationship project." We had to choose a challenging person in our lives and create a new relationship with them. I wanted to be free of the hatred and resentments associated with my mother, and this project was transformative in that process. Looking back, I can see the last ten years of caring for my aging mom were only made possible because of this soul-level educational experience.

I graduated the program—and even signed up for a third year of study in "Consciousness, Health and Healing"—without having missed a weekend and without debt. I was full of loving and a deeper sense of possibility.

20

Don't Fall

"I feel like I'm going to fall over when I close my eyes," she says to me, standing naked in the small shower area of the assisted living home. This weekly showering routine is nearing its end. I sit close by, ready to break her fall and catch her at any moment should she slip.

"Then don't close your eyes, Mom," I say. I am sitting in my manual wheelchair, which is wedged into the small bathroom, its metal push-rims scraping the tiled edge of the shower stall on one side. I'm boxed in securely between toilet and sink cabinet.

The burdens of caring for an aging parent are tough even for the average, able-bodied adult in the U.S. Statistics show I am in the "sandwich generation," so-called because adults in this age range often care for their children and parents at the same time. Luckily for me, I only have an aging parent—who sometimes acts like a child. I have to count my blessings as they appear. And because of the internal shifts and the skills I learned from USM, I can come into my relationship and this situation with kindness, patience and loving.

My mom works diligently to clean her thin, frail body, reaching down cautiously to scrub between toes, then lower legs, upper legs and the front and back of her genital area. She shivers as the water runs through her blond, grey-and-black-streaked hair, then cascades down over her thin, rounded shoulders. I marvel at how this eighty-two-year-old woman who can't remember what I said to her three minutes ago knows so well what to do; the ritual of human bathing has become embedded deep enough in her memory that she doesn't need to think about it.

"Okay here comes the shampoo, Mom," I say. "Close your eyes so you don't get stung by the soapy bubbles." I keep my tone gentle. I'm her helper now and have somehow by default been designated the person to get her into the shower. The assisted living personnel have all but given up, even though this is part of their job. She resists anyone but me helping her with this very personal and private activity.

My Mom was never a big fan of accepting help. She was always fiercely independent and worked many jobs to support five kids as a single mother. Because she divorced my father when I was eight years old—and subsequently divorced a step-father a few years later—I often took over the responsibility of parenting and disciplining my four younger siblings. I don't recall if my Mom ever specifically asked me to help; it was just assumed I would.

"Okay, I need the conditioner now," she commands me as the water rinses the shampoo from her hair. Her native New Yorker mannerisms are still present: blunt, straight and to the point, coming off as demanding. I rush to squirt the smooth, cloudy liquid across the top of her head before she gets too agitated at my delay. I should have been watching more closely; obviously my timing is a bit off.

As I sit in this cramped, humid enclosure, watching and ready for her to fall at any moment, I wonder how this aging process will continue to unfold for her. So far, except for intermittent confusion, poor short-term memory and increased anxiety, she is doing relatively well. She can still walk around with the use of a four-wheeled walker—even maneuvering carefully down the back-porch ramp for a cigarette break, skillfully lighting up that cigarette. She dresses herself appropriately for the weather. She knows when it's wine time, asking nicely for her daily allotment of two small bottles, sipping slowly to make it last a bit longer.

She also makes sure the resident cat is fed, watered and resting on her bed, and that the aging parakeet gets its seed and continues to chirp and liven up her room. She folds her blankets, tidies her space, and keeps everything in order.

In short, she's more than capable. In fact, she's always busy, as she has been her whole life. But at least now the busyness keeps her moving and attentive; perhaps she's not as productive in the grand scheme of things, but she is at least occupied and focused on her immediate surroundings in a positive way.

"Dear Blessed Mother, Dear Blessed Mother, Dear Blessed Mother, Dear Blessed Mother," she whispers over and over again as, shower finished, she dries the spaces between toes and the rest of her body. She works with diligence, calming herself with these swift short prayers to the blessed mother of Jesus. I'm not sure if this helps her anxiety or if perhaps the prayers are just the expressions of a highly charged internal state. She is afraid she'll fall, always bracing for the possibility and yet never hitting the ground.

I don't interfere. I just sit, watch and pray in silence that she doesn't fall off the plastic shower bench into the cramped stall.

In fact, I also pray for myself that she does not fall. In this tiny space, with the door shut behind my wheelchair, it would be difficult, if not impossible, for anyone to get into the room to help us in case of emergency. So, my prayer takes on these qualifying elements: *if* she falls, please, Dear Blessed Mother, let it happen in a larger room.

"Okay, I'm dry. What do I do now?" My mom is standing naked on a fuzzy blue throw rug, shivering, and I hand her a pajama shirt and a towel to wrap around her waist. She's done, but there's no room for me to back up and get out the door, so we face each other, only inches apart.

"Mom," I say gently, "please back up as far as you can against the wall so I can roll forward and open the door."

She backs up against the wall. I roll forward—so close to her that I am about to run over her toes. She presses her small self against the wall. I reach back with my left arm to turn the door handle, swing it open and then catch the edge of the door with my right hand and push it past the back of my wheels. I have to roll forward a bit and turn my front wheels to the right. Quite the contortionist act, to squeeze out of this tight space.

"Okay, got it," I say, relieved. I think she is relieved too, as her feet and toes are now free to move.

I back my wheelchair out the doorway and then across the hallway into her room. I keep my eyes on her. She looks both ways, as if crossing a street, before leaving the bathroom and walking carefully across the hall into her small bedroom.

"What do I do now? What do I put on?" Her anxiety is beginning to rise along with her confusion around these next steps of the dressing process.

"Your clothes are ready and out on the bed. Just sit down, and you can get dressed right here." I find my patience getting thin now. I have laid everything out. I try to make it easy for her. Everything is in putting-on order: bra and panties on top, then shirt, pants, socks and finally slippers.

She's still flexible enough to reach both arms around her back for the hook and loop of a standard bra, and she succeeds on her first attempt.

"Where's my deodorant and powder?"

"Right here, Mom." I push the blue deodorant case closer to her side and put the plastic bottle of powder directly into her outstretched hand. She applies both, and is now ready to pull on her long-sleeved shirt. The pants are pulled up as she stands at the bedside, with me close by for steadying.

She sits down and gets ready to pull on her socks, but then blurts out, "Ouch! My toes hurt so badly! You need to take me to a specialist."

I reach for the sharp clippers stored among the other personal care items. "I'll do your nails, Mom," I reply confidently. "I'm your specialist today." I've been clipping her nails for over a year. Positioning my wheelchair next to the bed, I lift her foot onto my lap and launch into the tricky task of clipping and shortening her irregular toenails, which strangely grow up vertically, not horizontally. I work my way around the softened nail tissue, clipping and shaving along the way, careful not to pinch or cut any toe flesh. She flinches, letting me know when I get too close to skin. I keep working at each nail, bit by bit, trimming them all down to a manageable level ready for socks, slippers and no pain. When I'm finished, she inspects each nail, feeling for rough, uneven edges until she deems the operation a success. Nails done. I throw the clippers back into the cup so that they're available for my next toenail specialist duties.

She's ready now for the hairbrush to run through her still-wet hair. Natural curls fall into order with the brushing and fluffing. She looks refreshed and clean. Almost done.

"What do I do now?" she asks again.

"Whatever you want, Mom. I'll put all the dirty clothes and towels in your hamper. I've got to go now and get to the store"

"Wait, wait. Just sit with me for a while," she says, sounding a little frantic.

"I've got to go, Mom. I'm sorry. I have some things I need to do for me today." I feel my patience thinning again. She seems to have no real sense of time or the effort it took to help her.

"Okay, okay," she says. "Thank you for helping me. I just want you to stay, please don't go."

I roll myself closer to the door and turn to leave. She reaches forward, hugs me and kisses my cheek. I head out of her room, down the hallway to the front door and out to my vehicle. Now my heavy lifting begins again, as I need to load myself and the wheelchair into the vehicle. I reach for the strap on the vehicle frame and pull myself to standing, then pivot and slide into the driver's seat. Finally, I load my wheelchair by taking off the two wheels, storing them in the back seat, and lifting the frame up and onto the passenger seat. I start the car, clip my seatbelt and shift into reverse, check the rearview mirror and back out of the parking spot.

Mom opens the front door and waves into the air, hoping I'll see her as I pull away. She looks clean, fresh and frail all at once. In a stark moment of clarity I see my aging Mom.

"Bye, Mom!" I yell back. And silently think to myself, *Dear Blessed Mother, Dear Blessed Mother, please don't let her fall.*

Because if she does, I won't be there to catch her.

21

Both Sides of the Bed Rail

Patient description: forty-five-
year-old female, injured in a single
vehicle rollover accident. Her
injuries include a teardrop fracture
of the C5 vertebra resulting in a
spinal cord injury, broken wrist,
fracture of the jaw and lacerations
to the face. Patient was reported to
have been observed by the emergency
room staff to be intoxicated; no
blood alcohol level provided.

I've been to this hospital before. The first time I arrived in the
back of an ambulance after being lifted from the roadway
following my accident. I came in through the emergency room
door and was rushed into a tiny exam room. Everything was a
blur, but I was still conscious.

This time, almost thirty years later, I feel conflicting
emotions. I remember the details of that day: the pain up my back,
the resulting paralysis of my legs—and the looming question of
whether I could continue life as an active young woman.

Back then I had been a patient; today I must take on my role as a nurse. In my accident, I was on my bike and the driver who hit me was drunk; today the patient I'm seeing was apparently drunk and caused the accident that resulted in her own paralysis.

I finish reading her report before unloading myself onto the blacktop of the hospital parking lot from my specially equipped VW van. I make sure my official Craig Hospital nametag is clearly visible and put on my professional face and demeanor.

My wheelchair glides smoothly and silently over the shiny, clean floors of the hospital. An elevator opens on my right and a big, grey trash cart stops abruptly; thankfully the worker sees me via the bubble mirrors on the ceiling. Many times in this wheelchair I've been inadvertently hit by people with their luggage, their kids and anything else that happens to be at that approximately four-foot-high level of space I inhabit. It's trained me to be very good at anticipating and avoiding collisions.

In the elevator up to the ninth floor, I quickly review the important issues I must attend to in my short visit with the patient. My job is to do an on-site, live evaluation of her physical condition, motivation for learning and post-rehab discharge placement. How much does she know about her injury? About paralysis and loss of sensation? What changes has she noticed in her injuries since the initial injury ten days ago? How is physical therapy going for her? What is her emotional state, and does she understand the blunt realities of her injury? What's her family situation, and does she have plans for relocating after completing rehab? And on and on.

I was in a similar boat at the time of my injury as I considered my own options for rehabilitation. I knew I needed to start on the road to recovery. I had no idea what that meant at the time.

Neither does my patient today. So in a way I'm grateful I've had my own firsthand experience of the fear and confusion she's feeling now, because it will help me help her.

Other people are in the elevator: there's a father and two young girls holding flowers and gifts; a hospital staffer, hot lunch in a to-go box; an older gentleman who seems to be trying hard not to look sad or afraid of what's on the other side of the elevator door. All of them look at me either sort of or not at all. I'm a curiosity, and I'm very familiar with that "look-but-don't-look" glance from people unsure of how to hold themselves around someone in a wheelchair. I just settle in and am kind to those around me who are experiencing their own pain in one way or another.

"Those are pretty flowers," I say to the girls, who smile

"These are for our mom. We have a new baby brother!" they say almost in unison. I'm warmed by the interaction. The children show a healthy curiosity. They're not yet afraid of someone who sits in a wheelchair. I am aware that perhaps I can help them know people in wheelchairs aren't to be feared; in fact, we can even be pleasant!

The father smiles back, perhaps thankful for his excited kids, or perhaps just relieved that the tension in the elevator has been broken.

Gradually the elevator crowd thins out, and by the time I reach the ninth floor I'm alone.

Next stop: nurses' station.

It's a professional courtesy to check in with the regular nurses of any patient. A worker at the station desk glances up at me.

I say, "I'm Terry Chase, Clinical Nurse Liaison from Craig

Hospital, here to evaluate the patient in 913. May I ask who her nurse is today? I have a few questions before I go in."

The healthcare worker scans the nurse assignments board, makes a quick call on the intercom, then returns to her work, leaving me to glance through paperwork and organize my thoughts some more.

Eventually the assigned nurse appears partway down a long hall to my right. She's just left another patient's room and is rubbing what I imagine is hand sanitizer over her palms. She waves them in the air to dry the last remnants off before taking my outstretched hand and introducing herself as Lorna.

I greet her back, smiling professionally.

"Hi, I'm Terry Chase, Clinical Nurse Liaison from Craig Hospital here to evaluate your patient in 913. Ms. Danvers." Lorna nods in recognition. "Do you have a few minutes so I can get some recent information, like today's vitals, and maybe your perspective on how she's doing?"

In the back of my mind is the thought, *I want you on my side going into the patient's room.* I don't want to be perceived as an interloper, or as stepping on anyone's toes. My role here is quite specific, and I make this clear by staying focused on what I need to know for a successful patient transfer. I want to support the efforts of my fellow nurses, who can often get left out of the important conversations, which is ironic—to say the least. Nurses have more direct contact with patients than virtually anyone else in a hospital, so naturally they usually know more about patients and their behaviors, as well as their responses to medicines and treatments.

"Okay, what do you need?" Lorna asks as we huddle close to

the computer screen. Lorna logs into a secure patient database and retrieves Ms. Danvers' record.

I pay attention not just to what's on the screen, but to what Lorna tells me—data alone is far less important without the insights of a nurse who knows the patient as well as their data.

I say, "I need a quick update on vitals for today, as well as anything you can tell me about the patient's behaviors and interactions." Lorna starts telling me what I want to know, and I follow up with more questions: "What do you observe when they're in therapy or learning new routines?" "How do they treat the staff?" "How about their bowel program and any skin issues?"

I am using both personal and professional experience with the rehabilitation process to ask some questions about the patients' chance for success in a demanding rehab program. I am looking for and listening to clues that will help me know if this patient has "what it takes" in the rigorous physical, occupational therapy and nursing program. Not only had I completed the spinal cord injury process, I directed the patient education program for eighteen years at Craig Hospital. Not everyone who gets admitted there takes full advantage of the opportunity for life-changing therapy and education for a healthy, happy life.

We speak with each other nurse to nurse, through the shared, unique, close-to-the-bedside experience of caring for those in pain, those who've lost body functions and who are on emotional rollercoasters.

Memories of those early days creep back, and I recall lying in the hospital bed, tubes running into and out of me, assisting with usual bodily functions. A stiff, uncomfortable body brace made of plaster kept my back straight and still while the backbones healed, held in place with hardware, screws, and metal shafts along my spine. Legs that were used to walking, running and jumping now lay still, covered by white sheets. I knew the physical experience of spinal cord injury. I knew, too, the inner wondering, questions and longing to be whole again. The middle of the night fears and crying times too.

This prompts my next question. "So how is the patient doing with all this? Is she motivated and realistic or struggling with the changes?" Emotional ups and downs are to be expected.

Of course, Ms. Danvers could be—probably is—both motivated and struggling. And more. There is no "usual" or "expected" way to deal with changes of this magnitude after a sudden and catastrophic injury. Our patient has a significant injury to her spine. Her hands and upper extremities no longer work well, and paralysis has taken away her fine motor skills.

"Oh, she's doing alright," Lorna tells me in a confidential whisper. "You know, some periods of tearfulness and sadness. She seems to be quite motivated, though. She has a young son, and he seems to be her focus for moving on."

"That's good," I reply, happy that Ms. Danvers has a powerful motivating factor in her life.

I know those periods of tearfulness and sadness extremely well. They swept over me late into the night, when no one else was around, overwhelming me with a sense of profound loss and sadness. My body so changed as to take away from me my freedom of movement. I'd had no young son to motivate me. But I *did* have my middle school students hoping I'd return as their PE teacher who loved to play alongside them.

Lorna is quietly looking from her notepad to the screen and

back again, which I take to mean she's probably covered everything. I say, "Anything else you'd like me to know before I go to her room?" I always do this, leaving space for any last facts or impressions that don't fit neatly into what's come before.

"No, I don't think so." She smiles at me. "I hope she gets to go to Craig Hospital. She'll do so well there. She's motivated, and maybe that'll help her get on with her life. I see so much potential in her."

"Yes," I reply, sensing I'm expected to say something more. "Sometimes these kinds of injuries do help a person get more focused and get on with their lives, and I hope that's the case for her. I'll check in with you when I'm done. Thanks so much for helping me with the details."

I gather my paperwork and my thoughts, readying myself for the face-to-face meeting with the patient I've only met "on paper." That's one big thing I've learned as a nurse: to be open to the experience of the person, not just the what the documentation tells me. Each patient has their own story to tell and for me to know about them. I head to Ms. Danvers room ready for the assessment to begin.

***

I didn't get a visit like this when I was a patient. What I got was a doctor coming into my room as I was coming out of a morphine haze, and hearing him say, "You need to decide where to go for rehab."

With very little warning I had to make a decision that would affect the rest of my life.

"What are my options?" I asked, grasping for some clarity as my mind swirled with the cocktail of medicines in my body.

"Well", he started, "your options are not many. You can stay here in town and go to the local rehab center." I knew about that local rehab center. They treated the elderly post-stroke, and people with hip replacements. That didn't sound like the place for a thirty-two year-old woman. "Or," the doctor continued, "you can go to this place called Craig. It's a hospital in Denver that specializes in treating people with spinal cord injuries. They've got a great rehabilitation program, not to mention more patients your age."

I had to make this decision on my own. I didn't have any family members with me, and I didn't think I could wait long to make up my mind, so I answered the doctor quickly, knowing that if I hesitated I might end up being sent to the local rehab center.

"I'll go to Craig Hospital," I said. "It sounds like a good place."

Little did I know that I'd just made the most important decision of my young life. I'd done it all alone and in a morphine haze—with more hope than trust or knowledge.

Thank God it turned out to be the right one for me.

And in my position now, and with a little luck, I'll be happy to help the patient in front of me to make the right decision for *her.*

***

The room is well-lit and bright, all surfaces clean at first glance. The patient is expecting me, as are the family members who've joined her for my visit. From the entrance I see the standard rolling table, call light, poles holding IV fluids and monitoring devices, and the standard pink washbasins. I take in at a glance the numbers on the monitor screen, how close the patient's utensils and cups are, and what she's reading from the stack of books and magazines on the tabletop. My sense of smell tells me about how recently she's had a bath or teeth-brushing.

But of course, I rely on the patient, currently lying in the bed beneath the hospital's stiff, white sheets and blanket, to give me the true picture.

"Hello," I gently call in as I tap on the heavy room door.

Now I adopt a demeanor that blends the professional and personal. I'm conscious that I'm moving into this patient's space. This is her room, her bed and her pain.

I roll slowly into the room, feeling confident. This is a world of professional nursing I've been part of for a while now.

The patient is sitting up; the upper part of the bed has been elevated. She's dressed in clean clothes and looks alert and ready for our conversation—there's certainly no hint of a morphine haze. The smells of soap, hand sanitizer and fresh linens permeate the air.

I greet her and her family members, knowing that seeing me arrive in a wheelchair takes some time to absorb and make sense of. I introduce myself and hear their names, knowing that this kind of familiarity can help normalize what can quickly become an emotionally complicated discussion.

I begin gently: "So tell me a little bit about your injury. I'd like to hear what you know. How would you say the spinal cord injury has affected your muscles and your ability to feel?"

I know for many people that having to say out loud how bad the body really is can be difficult, especially when family is present. But this patient speaks right up, displaying a sense of confidence in her knowledge and ability to tell like it is.

"Well, my legs don't work at all. I got my arms here—" she raises and lowers them to illustrate what she can do— "I don't have no finger movement. But," she adds, a hint of pride in her voice, "I can use the sides of my hands to press buttons and even dial my cellphone."

I can relate to everything she's doing. It was so important to me to be able to speak aloud and demonstrate what I could and couldn't do. I knew, just as this patient does, that when there's an awful lot that doesn't work, it helps to show what does.

"That's great," I reply. "What about sensation? Where can you feel or not feel on your skin surface?"

"Well, that's a problem." She lifts her arm and curled hand up to chest level and lets it hit her gently. "Up here, above my breasts, I can still feel like normal, but everywhere else— nothing." She lowers her eyes, almost as if ashamed, and looks away from me.

I get that too. When you expose your body and all its deficits to someone else, you also expose yourself to feelings of shame, even if that shame is pointless and undeserved.

"Thank you," I say, feeling genuine appreciation for her efforts and wanting to convey this through tone as well as words. "I appreciate your letting me know about this. You seem to have a really good sense of your body and where things aren't working as well—as difficult as that is to say out loud."

As the "professional" nurse, I could now just look in her chart, read the medical notes and find answers to my next questions, but this direct human connection is vital. I want to hear from the patient. I want to allow my intuition to blend with my professionalism to give me insights into how she's really handling this incredibly difficult time. I want to help her in a way I wasn't helped.

Basically, I want to do what I can to help her on a path towards to her fullest life—the kind of life I was afraid I'd never have when I was the patient on the other side of that bedrail.

So, after a brief pause to give her some time to regroup, we start discussing her move to rehab.

22

Welcome to America

I was a few weeks into my three-month externship rotation on the neurotrauma unit of Swedish Medical Center, in what was turning out to be my most intense learning experience to date as a nursing student. I'd completed year three of the doctorate program, and after this rotation I was set to take the registered nurse licensure exam and begin a year-long residency next door at Craig Hospital.

While I was assigned to the neurotrauma unit, patients rarely if ever questioned my capability. Maybe my being in a wheelchair made them more comfortable. I was not standing above them; I was sitting at eye level, equalizing our relationship from the start. I had four patients at Swedish whom I looked after with my nursing preceptor, Deb.

This particular morning we were meeting to discuss a particular patient's case with the other members of his healthcare team.

We shuffled into the conference room and took our places at the table. I had learned early on in my rotation that I was working with an experienced team. Most had been caring for the severely injured patients on this unit for over a decade. Dr. Joseph, a middle-aged attending physician, relied on the physical, occupational, and respiratory therapists, nursing staff and a social worker to provide high-quality care plans. Barbara, the social worker who now set a large binder and chart on the table, was very experienced and seemed to carry the weight of difficult decisions on her broad shoulders.

I sat next to Deb and waited for my turn to speak. Something had been heavy on my mind, and I wanted to share it.

This meeting had been called to discuss one of our most severely incapacitated patients. Bin was a twenty-four-year-old Chinese man who had come to America looking for freedom. He had taken a boat across the Pacific Ocean from China to California, then made his way to Colorado—where he was subsequently arrested as an illegal immigrant and placed in a detention center. After weeks of being held without expectation of release, he had apparently decided to end his life: guards found him hanging in his cell, a rolled-up shirt tied around his neck. They cut him down and worked to revive him. Following immediate emergency care, his heart was still beating, and he breathed on his own. Yet severe brain damage—anoxic brain injury, which occurs when the brain is deprived of oxygen for too long—left him in a vegetative state.

My preceptor and I had been assigned to care for Bin. He had been transferred to the neurotrauma unit for end-of-life care; this was not an injury he could recover from. So our treatment consisted of handling all his basic needs of nutrition, elimination, hygiene, and human contact.

Bin was one of the first of several "complicated" patients I'd be assigned during this externship. Already my nursing skills and confidence had grown as I'd been learning how to handle severely ill patients and the intense treatments they required.

When it was my turn to speak, I said, "If we get a call arranged with the family, I want to be sure they have a chance to talk to him for the last time."

The team looked at each other with questioning glances. I imagined their thoughts: "What is she talking about? He can't hear them. Besides, she's only a nursing student. What does she know?"

I was quite used to getting those kinds of looks, being a nursing student in a wheelchair. But today it was for a different reason. What I knew was that Bin's parents needed to speak to him, and he needed to hear them on whatever level possible. Fortunately I had become very used to the judgments from other healthcare providers in my student nursing position, so it was easier than it might have been to resist them.

"You know he's comatose, right?" Barbara said, her voice tinged with fatigue and emotion. She sat at the head of the table, looking stern and concerned, her pen poised above a pad of paper, ready to take notes and document any important decisions that were made. I knew she was simply looking out for her patients, having already witnessed firsthand her fierce determination and advocacy in other meetings. But today was a particular challenge, because it seemed there were no good options for the patient.

I remembered the sadness I'd felt at the injury that had taken away my basic capabilities, how I'd had to reclaim my voice, speak up and make my needs known. If I hadn't, no one else would have known what I was feeling and what I needed. Now Bin had no voice, and although our situations weren't identical, I wanted to help him connect with his world.

My heart racing, my throat tight, I leaned forward and spoke directly to Dr. Joseph. "Yes, I know... But... It's important even for a comatose patient to be spoken to directly. Studies have shown that patients who are unconscious can hear, and there is no definitive evidence indicating it's not useful." My palms were sweating and I feared being chastised as sentimental and impractical. But I stood firmly in what I believed was the right thing to do: advocate for a patient who could not speak for himself. "It's important for Bin and his family to have a word between themselves in his own language, not through an interpreter. I want him to be present while we discuss his options with his family."

It was only a moment before Dr. Joseph said with authority, "Okay I agree." He gave me a slight nod and a half-smile. "Let's get that phone call arranged as soon as possible. His prognosis is grim. He could live for an exceedingly long time, requiring 24/7 care in a facility skilled to handle the feeding tube, medications, and mobility. Or he could die within a week if we remove the tubes. We also have to take into consideration quality of life issues."

The team members around the table shifted in their chairs.

Barbara said, "His elderly parents and family live in a very rural part of China. They'll travel to take a phone call. I'll arrange for an interpreter to help them understand his condition, and we'll ask them for their wishes and determine what to do going forward."

The phone call with Bin's parents was arranged more quickly than we expected. Within a week I was helping get him ready for the meeting. I washed his face and hands, applied lotion and combed his straight, black hair. I made sure his feet were flat on the wheelchair footrests and that the shorts he was wearing fit comfortably on his slender legs. "You gotta look good for your family, Bin!" I said.

Bin had no reaction, just a vacant, blank stare. He was lost in a world of his own, and from our outside perspective he had no functional brain activity, no ability to communicate, and probably no awareness of the gravity of the phone call that was about to take place.

I double-checked that the feeding tube connected to a portal in his abdomen was not tangled or bent. The urinary catheter, which was attached to a large bag, was unobstructed. A protective adult diaper was in place in case of a bowel movement.

If Bin had been aware of these invasive and undignified measures to keep him alive at the age of twenty-four, he would most likely have been embarrassed. My own memories of being a patient were never far from my mind. Even though my injuries were far less severe, the dependence on others and the tubes and equipment I needed to assist me with basic bodily functions were constant reminders of a life rearranged.

I rolled slowly alongside Bin in his wheelchair through the hospital halls until we reached the conference room. Barbara was already there, dressed in a formal pantsuit. I knew she had worked diligently with the U.S. State Department, the U.S. Embassy in China and Bin's family to arrange this call. Interpreters were already in place with the parents.

I had no illusions that this would be a typical family conference call. Bin's parents were about to learn for the first time that their son was injured beyond recovery and unable to take care of himself. Furthermore, the medical, legal and financial issues involved in transferring him back to China made that option all but impossible.

The rest of Bin's healthcare team, dressed in their usual hospital scrubs and white uniforms, filed into the conference room to take their seats, saying "Hello" or touching Bin's hand in passing; his wheelchair was parked at the head of the table just inside the door. I sat next to him. A large black phone sat in the center of the table.

Barbara said, "We're having a little bit of trouble connecting to China. The circuits are busy, and the signal strength is not all that good."

Bin's breathing was light and steady as we continued to wait for the call to go through. I watched him, wondering if anything was going on in his mind. Communicating with him was always a one-way street; at best we noted occasional slight body movements and an inconsistent change in facial expression that may have had nothing whatsoever to do with an awareness of the outside world.

Finally, the call went through, and Barbara interrupted the small talk around the table to say, "Okay, we have them on the line. The interpreters are present, and Bin's mother and father are there."

"Good morning. I'm Barbara, the social worker here at Swedish Medical Center in Denver, Colorado." She introduced the rest of the team members by name and title, explained the purpose of the call, and let Bin's parents know why we were calling. Finally, she asked if they would introduce themselves as well, and then gave the floor to Dr. Joseph.

The interpreter translated the complicated medical terms and Bin's condition to the parents, who listened quietly. I wondered if the words they heard were even understandable in translation. His parents were farmers and peasants in a rural district of mainland China; they probably had very little if any experience with the complicated and terrible condition of their son.

The team members were kind and spoke slowly as they related details about Bin, explaining that he needed constant medical attention, nursing care and specialized equipment to keep him alive, and that the tools to do this in rural China were non-existent.

At one point Dr Joseph spoke up again, saying something to the effect that Bin had very few options. He could be moved to a long-term nursing facility, where his quality of life would be minimal. He told Bin's parents, "You would have to come to the U.S. to see him. Unfortunately I can't predict how long he might live in this vegetative state." After a pause he said, "I know this is difficult for you. You might also consider withdrawal of life-sustaining procedures. He is breathing on his own. If we removed him from life support, we would discontinue his feeding tube and water. Without these, he will slowly succumb to death. We would make sure he was comfortable with pain medications. His gradual withdrawal from life support might take several days or weeks. He is young, so his body will hold on for a while. The nursing team will tend to his physical needs and ensure his comfort." He paused again to let this information sink in, then ended with,

"What would you like us to do for your son?"

There was silence on the other end of the line, and silence in the hospital conference room.

Throughout the call I had been touching Bin's hand with warmth and caring, knowing he was not able to hear, much less process, the words being spoken. Then, as I watched his face, I felt an energy rise up in me and I said, "Is now a good time to give the family an opportunity to speak to Bin? This may be their last chance."

"Oh, of course," Barbara said. "Here. Let's get that phone over to the end of the table. Terry would you please hold the phone to Bin's ear so they may speak privately?"

I held the receiver as Bin listened to his family for the last time. The conversation in Chinese was barely audible from where I sat, yet I heard enough to know what was being expressed from the other side of the world. Bin's parents were saying goodbye to their son. The wrenching sadness of their voices was loud and clear, even without my understanding the words.

Not long after, the phone call ended.

The family had asked to discontinue life support and allow Bin to pass. They requested a cremation as the final step in his care.

Dr. Joseph removed his glasses and wiped his eyes, allowing a few minutes for all of us to regain our composure. Then he said, "As I told his parents, his body is strong, and as a young man this may take a while. We must monitor his pain and discomfort and be sure to administer medication appropriately."

The silence continued until I spoke up again. "Who will claim his ashes?"

There hadn't been any discussion during the call about having the ashes sent to China—whether that was due to the cost or it just not being part of their end-of-life practices, I do not know.

Barbara's voice sounded tired when she responded to me; I had the impression she was emotionally and physically exhausted from the call. "I don't know. Since he doesn't have any family or guardians in the U.S., they might just have to stay at the crematorium."

I said, "I'd like permission to pick up his ashes. I'll make sure they're properly cared for. He needs to have that dignity even after death."

Barbara was getting used to my requests. There was an unspoken bond between us now: we were both fierce advocates for those who could not speak for themselves.

"The permission to retrieve his ashes is noted," she said softly, writing a note in Bin's large chart. "Once they're ready for pick-up, Miss Chase, you will be the first to know. Thank you for taking care of this situation. I am sure the family will be grateful."

With this final point resolved, the nursing assistant rolled Bin's wheelchair out of the conference room. I followed, as did the rest of the team.

***

The end-of-life procedures were put into place. Over the course of the next week, Bin succumbed to the depletion of nutrients. He died in the middle of the night, peacefully. I was relieved to know he was at peace, no longer suffering in a body with little function. To have cared for him through to his end was a gift above and beyond the technical skills and specialized procedures I learned during this intense period of my training.

A few weeks after Bin's death, I picked up his ashes. I had a plan in mind.

Jones Pass is located fifty miles west of Denver at an elevation close to ten thousand feet—above the tree line, where the air is cold and brisk. Sharon and I drove there along a rough, rocky road in four-wheel drive, our dogs along for the ride, looking eagerly out the windows.

We reached a clearing and unloaded my wheelchair, and I maneuvered along the rocky mountaintop, looking for the exact right place to perform this ceremony. Honoring the solemnity of the day, I said a short prayer and a few words about Bin and his journey. I acknowledged his efforts to make it to freedom, then opened the plastic box and pulled out a small, clear-plastic bag of ashes.

As I looked out at the beautiful view of forest and mountains stretching into the distance, it occurred to me that I understood a new aspect of the theory of human caring: that the practice of patient care can extend even beyond a patient's death.

I undid the twisty-tie and turned the bag upside down. As the ashes swirled up into the fresh mountain air, I shouted to the wind, "Welcome to America!"

Spoke 3

23

They Bring Me Alive

I ride good today. Sitting tall in the saddle, jaw and face relaxed, trusting the horse, thirty minutes around the dry, dirt floor of the indoor arena. I concentrate with focused attention, supple muscles keeping this half-paralyzed body on the copper-colored back. "Head in the middle and a leg on each side," the old cowboy used to say. It's good advice, especially for me.

My body is tough, but fragile.

I didn't always feel this way on a horse. The injury took my legs out from under me, took away my ability to run, walk and climb mountains, and stole that tomboy swagger. But riding horses shook up my stuck emotional parts and helped rearrange them in a more cohesive, whole way. I became a better human being with the help of horses. They kept me present, in the here and now, totally real, and authentic. With their assistance, I found my voice and my power, and I created the path to my future.

The horses I'll introduce to you in the following pages have been my teachers for many years of learning and riding. All had previous working lives: some were champions in reining or cow-chasing or roping. In their old age, they became my teachers.

24

Sarge

My fascination with horses began in my teenage years, a time when most girls tend to fall in love with boys or horses—or both.

I was sixteen and the horse was Sarge. He needed care and regular feeding, and I was happy to take on that responsibility. Sarge belonged to a Nevada State Patrolmen who did not have time for the necessities of horse ownership. The patrolman was a frequent customer at the local A & W Drive-in where I worked as a carhop. In my conversations with him I somehow ended up volunteering to step in and help with his horse.

The first day I went out to Sarge's stable I received a quick, one-hour lesson on how to catch, halter, and lead him from pasture—as well as a bit or two about how to ride this big, fifteen-hand sorrel quarter horse. Then the patrolman went to work, and Sarge and I were on our own.

Daily responsibilities included feeding, filling water tanks, watching for problems, and an occasional ride in the pasture on the backside of Reno, Nevada—a town famous for gambling, casinos, cowboy culture and untamed spirit.

Sarge was a gentle giant. I struggled to reach his high head and put the halter on. We would walk together as friends back to the gate. I told him about my day as I cleaned the stall and made sure his feed was prepared properly. He just stood there calmly and listened in a horse kind of way. I was a busy teenager and those moments with Sarge were the only quiet times in my day.

But one day he had other plans with our routine. I was in a hurry and had to get to my carhop job. I whistled for him so we could get on with the usual chores. He remained just out of reach. No catching him today. I was impatient and needed to go. I got angry. I swung the halter and lead rope at him, smacking him across his back and big rear end. He moved quickly this time—but in the wrong direction.

This uncooperative beast had stirred up some hidden anger. At the same time I felt waves of guilt wash over me for having been so mean. Sarge missed his meal, and I missed my time with Sarge. I drove off to work with many conflicting emotions.

The next day, full of remorse and sorrow for having struck out at Sarge in anger, I was looking for forgiveness.

I approached; he looked up.

His eyes were full of kindness, and he lowered his head for the halter, then walked easily beside me. Sarge never again resisted. And I vowed to never again in my life to take my anger out on him or anyone else in a physical way. That was not the way I wanted to live. Up until then the only examples of rage and anger came from my chaotic home life, where hitting, beatings and screaming were all I knew. I did not want to carry this mindset with me through life, and my afternoons with Sarge opened me up to a quite different way of handling emotions in life.

Nonetheless, I carried the guilt of my action with Sarge for many years after.

***

"Sarge, I don't know, man. These cold, blustery Nevada winters are getting tough. You feel that cold wind, buddy?" His thick, brown coat kept him warm enough, and the shelters broke the blasting wind—but it was getting *cold.*

"I'm cold. You know? And tired. These late nights working at the A & W are getting to me. I have more homework too. I don't know, Sarge, I may not be able to keep coming out." It was a very hard decision to make. I did not want to stop caring for this gentle teacher, but something had to give. My young life was getting more hectic with working many hours during the week to help the family finances and caring for younger siblings in a chaotic household with an alcoholic mom. I had to make the decision to save myself. I was balancing way too many things for a sixteen-year-old, and I had no one to watch my back or tell me to slow down.

This would be the first of many hard decisions I would have to make, and I felt that Sarge had given me the strength and support to make this one. I knew he would understand. I told his patrolman owner well in advance and made sure someone else would take over his care.

So, when winter gave way to spring, I gave up my duties with Sarge and left this important relationship. He had become a beacon of kindness and patience and had taught me to handle anger in a better way. From that time on, I felt emotionally safe around horses and experienced a powerful sense of connection with them.

25

Breath and Body—Here and Now

As I completed one training program, another came into view, this time involving horses. The Gestalt-Equine Psychotherapy training program was developed by Duey Freeman. Gestalt-Equine Psychotherapy is a therapeutic approach integrating Gestalt therapy with a unique and powerful partnership with horses. Through the program we would learn—among many other things—how horses are masters of non-verbal communication. They are always in the moment, always focused on individual survival and the safety of the herd.

The two-year program offered a dual approach to learning through experiential Gestalt therapy sessions and horsemanship: riding, groundwork, grooming, nutrition, proper equine care, and handling. In short, combining the therapy with the horse as a partner offered a horse-human-therapist encounter.

It didn't matter that I used a wheelchair or walked with crutches. I wanted it—all of it: the intensive two-year learning commitment, the riding and involvement with horses, the challenge of pushing myself beyond any limitation. I already had two-years training in the Gestalt approach, so I appreciated the emphases of this program: self-awareness and working on what disturbed my ability to be in full contact or relationship with another human being. The core aspect of this work was experiential and expressive.

***

"Okay," Duey asks as our small group of trainees gathers in the arena. "Who'll be the client for this next session? Terry? You ready to jump in this time?"

Over the course of the four-day intensive training weekends we all take turns as client and therapist—experiential learning at its best. The horses are always part of the sessions.

"Sure, I'm up for that. I can come up with something to work on—though I'm not really feeling anything right now." I say this knowing full well that it isn't important to know, just to be open with what comes forward. I push my wheelchair through the soft sand to the arena gate, struggling yet again to keep up as we approach the horse.

William offers to be the therapist this time. He's recently graduated with a Master's in Counseling Psychology. He's a nice, quiet guy, low-key and kind. We've worked together in previous sessions. I trust him.

William and I meet at the gate of the arena. "Okay, Terry, let's start with just noticing your body and any sensations that are present now. Take a few breaths and let that exhale really lengthen." He speaks in a low, soft voice. I'm breathing heavily now from the exertion of pushing uphill through sand. I'm also aware of a slight but noticeable anger rising in me at having to struggle so much to be a participant in these sessions. This feeling still comes and goes at times, triggered by my sense of limitation and my frustration at being seen in my chair. Perhaps it also grows out of concern that others will see me as less than fully capable.

After over a year working with horses in the program I am beginning to be aware of my disconnection from my own feelings—but I'm still not always sure what to do with this awareness.

I roll into the arena and push a little closer to the horse who will be part of our team. She is an older bay, with a darker brown coat and a black mane. I recognize her from the herd that gathers around the fence line when we start our days at Star Peak Stables. The horses are becoming accustomed to seeing me in the wheelchair or hobbling around on my crutches. They've determined I'm not a threat and relax around me. Of course, they don't judge me for being half-paralyzed. And perhaps because of this, in their presence I feel whole again. I get out of my head and into my body.

The horses themselves model this grounded state of presence and authenticity. They've opened a new body of knowledge to me, a new way of life connected to nature, and a relationship that is deep and healing. They've woken me up.

"Here, Terry, take the lead rope. You and this horse are partners in this process." William hands me the rope. I touch the horse at the shoulders, feeling the soft, warm hair. I whisper a greeting to her and ask her permission to come a bit closer. She shuffles slightly and lowers her head, ears turned toward me. We exchange glances. For now, I feel connected to her, and it's safe to begin the session.

William says, "Tune into the sensations in your body. Starting at the top of your head and moving slowly down through your shoulders, back, mid-section, legs and feet, just notice. Take your time. Remember we're on horse time today. No need to hurry."

"Okay, sure," I say—through slightly clenched teeth and jaw. What I'm thinking is, *I don't want to feel.* I am pissed and hot and angry at having to always struggle with this wheelchair and having to keep up with these strenuous aspects of the program.

William stands by, breathing calmly and in no hurry. He's playing the therapist role quite well. The horse, on the other hand, begins to pull away and indicates an interest in something at the fence.

"I'm not feeling anything," I say, holding the lead rope a bit tighter as the horse puts her weight into changing directions and walking away. I cannot physically control the horse just by strength alone, and for sure I am no match pound for pound.

"What are you noticing now, Terry?" William just stands there, not helping me at all.

"Well, it's obvious the horse is pulling away from me. I'm holding on tight and she's not paying attention to me." I am gritting my teeth, and I imagine my frustration is starting to show.

"Express it out loud, Terry. Say what's true for you right now. Sure, it's obvious what the horse is doing, but what's going on inside *you*?"

Suddenly the lingering anger wells up and the tears begin to flow. I am holding onto this large beast of a horse to get it to stay right *here*, but it's not working. Slowly but surely, the horse is dragging me with her.

"I'm angry," I say quietly, but my voice gets louder and less restrained as I go on. "I am upset. I am tired of being in this *&@#$ wheelchair. I am tired of not keeping up with the class. I am struggling to control this horse!"

I'm crying now, wailing. Deep screams of anger and hurt that have been stuffed down for so long. My hold on the horse lightens up, the lead rope goes limp in my hand.

But the horse has turned back to face me.

My crying continues for many more minutes. I speak out loud the disgust I hold for myself in this broken body. I shout to the hills my desire to climb and walk them again. My body feels limp—but gradually I notice it's also starting to feel refreshed at the same time, cleansed. The horse has joined me, and she never leaves my side. In fact, she leans toward me with each scream and expression.

The horse is teaching me an amazing, powerful lesson. Horses need congruence, a state where the inside emotions match the outward expression of them. I understand this unequivocally now.

I share these raw emotions with the horse in the sandy, outdoor arena. The shadows grow longer as the afternoon sun starts to fall behind the mountain peaks. It comes to me that, in essence, I am unconditionally accepted by the horse. And this helps me accept myself.

After a long while I feel better, more grounded, more real. I say to William, "Thank you, William. That was a really important session. Thank you for holding the space." After letting that sink in, I add, "Really though, this horse was my therapist!"

We sit in silence a little longer, then William asks, "Terry, how will you use this learning going forward? Is there anything that you'll take with you beyond the arena into your life?"

I sit deep in my wheelchair, feeling supported by the backrest, holding the lead rope across my lap, watching the long afternoon shadows creep across the dirt. Feeling relaxed, safe and whole again, I say, "Holding my anger inside is not the way to go forward. It only hurts me and keeps me stuck. I've done that with all my emotions, and it makes it hard for me to feel joy and love in my life. This horse let me know it's okay to express what is true for me. This is what I'll take forward with me. I have to, actually: it's in my body now."

And it's true.

This is a turning point for me, coming as it does midway through the two-year program. I finally understand what it means to experience the powerful healing capacity of horses.

26

Learning to Ride

Horsemanship training was held at Star Peak Stables, a high-elevation horse ranch effectively dug into a mountainside. There was not much level ground on which to roll my wheelchair—only the concrete pad with a hitching post for the horses. Of course, I wasn't there to roll around in my chair; I was there to ride. At first I didn't realize just how much I would learn about myself in the process.

"Ready to ride?" Julia asked our small group, then looked up at me in the saddle on the first day of riding instruction as part of the Gestalt-equine training program. Julia Clavette was my trainer at Star Peak Stables; she had a lifetime's worth of horse experience and a strong teaching background. I'd been in and out of relationships with horses since I was sixteen, but I'd never had a riding lesson, much less ridden with other people in an arena.

Those early rides in the program were revealing. I didn't know much about riding horses. I was riding western style, like the old cowboys of rugged Nevada and my early days with Sarge, Julia made a quick assessment of my lack of skills and confidence. She calmly adjusted the lessons to fit my beginner level and selected horses that were old-school trained and reliable. She kept working with me and helped me through the rough times without a hint of judgment or scolding.

"Sure," I said. "I'm ready!" There was no hint in my voice of the fear and panic that rose in me as surely as the kicked-up dust from the dry earth rose into the hazy sunlight—our group horse-riding lessons were held in a sandy outdoor arena.

"Start slow, everyone. Keeping your horses at a walk around the arena. Breathe. Relax the shoulders, loosen your jaw muscles, sink into the saddle. The horses will know when you're present with them. They need the connection with you to feel safe." Julia spoke with the firm but kind voice of someone who really knew how to work with people and horses.

I felt small and out of place amongst the other riders. Most of my classmates had years of horse experience and had no problems in this rugged place. I was none of these things. Often I gave into the habit of shrinking into my wheelchair and retreating inside myself. As always I was determined to counter this impulse, to hold myself bigger than the chair. In my efforts to do so, I had made myself appear so big that I hoped nobody really saw how small I felt inside.

Yet when I was with horses, I never felt the *inside* smallness that was so familiar. I had no need to shrink or hide myself. The horses could not have cared less that I was in a wheelchair or walking unsteadily on crutches. The horses met me where I was—literally. A horse's nose found me at chest level, and our eyes met just above the horizon. I could usually reach all areas of them for brushing and cleaning, except perhaps for the tallest of horses.

Sure, they needed a little bit of time to get used to the wheelchair. Very soon their natural curiosity kicked in, and then their noses would approach the custom-made cushion, sniffing with curiosity, and nibbling a bit. Once they made sure the chair was not some kind of unconventional predator, there was no concern or doubt.

I respected their size, knowing a sudden or unexpected movement would startle them. I moved deliberately and intentionally, and always let the horse know where I was by touch or soft words.

I gradually began to trust myself and the horses. Over the two-year program, I made gains in my riding abilities. I sometimes went backwards in my ability for no apparent reason except—I discovered—that I had lost confidence in myself and crumpled inside. Some days when my pull on the reins was too hard and sharp or my tapping on the horse's side was not crisp and definitive, the horse would not respond. If my request for a stop was not clear, the horse would just walk on.

On days when fatigue and the weight of the world felt heavy on my shoulders, I wanted to let the horse lead. I quickly learned this didn't work well. The horse simply met my energy level. It responded to my subtle cues—which were sometimes so subtle that even I didn't notice them. My whole body and mind had to trust the horse; if I sat too rigid or off-center, the horse would be confused. And in turn, I could get off-center and twisted up if I did not monitor or pay attention to what the horse was doing. If I didn't lead in a session, the horse would simply stop moving.

I learned about leadership from within, about raising my own energy up and taking charge. I learned about pressure and release, about looking where I wanted to go and applying pressure in specific ways to direct the horse. Releasing pressure signaled positive acknowledgement of doing the right thing. I became sensitive to the horse's responses. The awareness I gained from them about the pressure of my touch, my voice, my presence, made me softer and more loving.

I was hard on myself. I gradually learned that my self-judgement and negative thought patterns just made things harder. They interfered with my ability to relax with the horse—who sensed this and then resisted me. I came to realize that my thoughts were more powerful than even my half-paralyzed body. Once I started to let go of my thinking and get out of my head, riding horses became far more relaxed and natural.

"Relax your jaw," Julia would say repeatedly. "Pull those shoulders down and back. Take your time. Breathe as you warm up. The horse will relax as you relax."

Breath. A simple function that keeps us alive, yet such a complex and powerful vehicle for calming the entire body. Horses know if I'm holding my breath—and they sense there might be something to be afraid of. Amazingly, despite the massive size and power of these animals, I've learned to breathe steadily and calmly in order to help the horse be calm as well.

Gradually, then, something shifted in me when I got on a horse. My attitude lifted. I learned to simply *be*. I was authentic with myself. If I was scared, I could simply *be scared*. If I was tired, I could *be tired*. I did not have to fight those feelings in myself. There was a natural feedback between me and the horse. Whenever I wasn't real with my emotions, my riding did not go well. If I allowed myself to accept my fears and be scared in the moment, my time with the horse was far more fluid and satisfying. I remembered the lesson learned from Sarge so long ago. I was never angry at the horse, never took out any frustration on it.

I just got to be real with the horses. Really I had no choice: there was no fooling them. There were many rides around the arena when my tears flowed and my sadness was held by the horse. And there were times of great joy, where I was filled with confidence.

The physical power of the horses has transformed and healed me. As I ride, the rhythmic pulses from a trotting horse's muscular gait travel up through my legs and torso and my back muscles ache from the workout. As that kinesthetic experience flows through me, sensations of movement and power course through my body, and I feel connected to the earth. The horse is my partner, and I'm incredibly grateful for it. Every time I slide off its back I say "thank you" as I pat its warm belly.

27

Keep Riding. Keep Learning.

"Let's do the high trail ride today," Julia said as we prepared the horses for another lesson. At this point I'd been riding and learning from Julia and her horses for over a decade. Riding horses had become a huge part of my life.

I had been working on the low trail ride many times over the course of the summer. Now, apparently, it was time to graduate upwards. I wasn't sure I was ready.

"Sure, let's do it," I said, pushing past a trickle of anxiety. I would be riding Badir, a sturdy mare whom I had ridden for many years now. We had done well together as a team, and I trusted her.

I knew the lower part of the ride well: out of the property to the dirt road, then through a kind of enchanted forest (as Julia called it), a short piece of softened path winding through a dense patch of pines, with a carpet of dry needles and soft moss sliced by beams of sunlight. Then up the rocky path to the back of the pasture.

The new path led us through more forested areas. When we

reached the pasture we headed left and started up the mountainous terrain, which took us through tall green pines and shimmering aspens. The horses followed the familiar (to them) path upward, stepping carefully over fallen tree limbs and branches. Eventually we rode up above the tree line, over the ten-thousand foot mark of elevation. The forest gave way to open sky and rock, and we soon came to a small pond created by melting winter snow. Walking slowly into the cold, shallow water, Badir felt comfortable and familiar beneath me, but I still held my breath as we made our way into the middle of the pond. Swirling in my head were thoughts of everything that could go wrong.

What if she gets nervous and bucks me off?

What if she slips on the rocks?

What if, what it, what if?

And so it went, on and on and on.

Badir knew this pond and the surrounding area well. Nothing happened.

Well, that's not true. What *happened* was that I relaxed. I felt the familiar sensation of being high up in the mountains. Memories flowed from the times I had walked forests and hills and mountains like these as a mountaineering instructor. I didn't realize how much I had missed the mountain air and the scent of the surrounding trees.

What happened is that as I sat atop Badir, embraced by the natural world in the melt pond, feeling so confident and comfortable, *I came back to myself.*

Many years of rides in the arena, diligent practice, growing competence and confidence, led to increasing challenges and increasing skills: walking and trotting the horse over poles on the ground, turning the horse around in a circle in an eight-foot box, increasing our gait from walking to trotting . . . and then finally riding over backcountry trails through high alpine meadows.

All this learning took place with horses named "Slick," "Symphony," "Peaches," "Pi," "Scooter," "Fairplay," "Star," "Badir" and "Salsa"—all of whom helped me find my balance and graciously forgave my ineptitudes. They helped me claim a newfound steadiness on their backs, while at the same time I *re*claimed my inner strength. All that time, all that practice, bit by bit, hour by hour, horse by horse—an investment of time and money in myself that proved to be of immeasurable value.

Because the horses helped me find myself again.

28

A Slice of Pi

I am participating in the very first competitive horse show of my life.

I get up early and roll outside onto the back porch, a cup of steaming black coffee in hand, feeling the cool, brisk, early spring air on my face. I want to be ready, fully awake and alert for the big day. I've competed in many sporting events in my life, but never as a horseback rider in an arena by myself.

I've entered a local event in the Para-Equestrian Western Dressage division. The test is called "Novice Level 1a," which is appropriate, because I am truly a novice. And of course, I'm truly a paraplegic as well—hence the "para-equestrian" designation.

A quick, light breakfast, and then on to dressing. I consider my clothing carefully. Do I wear the lighter blue-patterned dress shirt with fancy, square-button snaps? Or the darker pink one with long sleeves, a tiny horseshoe pattern and plaid collar, again with snaps for buttons and cuffs?

I want to look like a real cowgirl. One of the requirements of the western dressage event is western attire. So given my light blue jeans, I think the long-sleeved pink shirt will be better offset by the black vest and my brown riding boots, which fit comfortably with the plastic ankle-foot-orthotic braces stabilizing my paralyzed lower extremities. It's funny, in a way; I'm worrying about what the judges will think of my dressing choices, but they'll be sitting at the far end of the arena, not even close enough to see the horse hair and barn dust on that favorite black vest of mine.

I'm excited, maybe even a bit nervous, but it's not that *serious* nervousness I felt eight years ago when I first started riding horses, shortly after the death of my father. His passing shook me to my core. Those early days of learning to ride were marked by fear, a lack of confidence in myself and the grief and sadness of losing him so unexpectedly.

For over a year now, a new horse named Pi has been my partner. Pi is a twenty-year-old Polish Arabian mare, highly trained and decorated in many western events, including reining, the Arabian games and dressage. Her color is officially chestnut, but I say she looks like a newly minted copper penny, especially in the sunshine. Her mane is highlighted with grey, lending her a sophisticated and regal look.

***

I arrive at the fairground arena an hour before the appointed showtime. Our event is officially scheduled for 9:12 a.m.—not a minute sooner, and certainly not a minute later. Pi and I have been practicing this particular western dressage pattern for only two weeks. It's the novice level test done at a walk, no trotting. I hope to remember the proper sequence of straights, turns, circles and half circles, and to guide this experienced and trusted horse through the course without a single mishap or wrong turn.

Pi gets to the event early, along with another horse named Zeb. When I arrive I find them both in the parking lot with Jenn, my riding instructor. Pi is waiting patiently, tethered to the outside of the trailer, alert and attentive to the sights and sounds of this busy place. Horse trailers and trucks fill the parking lot, and crowds of people and horses bustle about in preparation for the upcoming day. I say Pi's name softly while rolling my wheelchair towards her through the mud created by the early morning rain. I keep myself within her line of vision, slightly off-center, knowing how important it is to not surprise a horse. Pi is used to the wheelchair, and it doesn't bother her.

Horses can get used to many different things as long as the horse thinks they are safe. Horses are prey animals, so they're always on the lookout for a predator.

This morning Pi nickers softly to me, probably hoping for a horsey treat. Horses like to eat, and given the opportunity they'll do so for sixteen to eighteen hours a day. Pi is always on the ready for food.

For the moment I push past her and continue across the muddy lot to the open side of the long horse trailer. Here I locate the box of brushes and utensils used for horse cleaning. Back by her side, I touch Pi softly on the shoulder with my bare hands, feeling her smooth coat and morning warmth. I want us to share that personal contact first, before beginning the task of grooming. I want her to know I'm here, and that I appreciate her being here too. Then I find the soft bristle brush and begin grooming. I reach way up to where the blanket and saddle will be placed, and in long, rhythmic strokes, brush away the dirt, dust and remnants of hay while talking softly with her about our upcoming event.

Horses can clearly read non-verbal cues. I let Pi know I'm a little scared, this being my very first horse show and all. I know it's best to be honest with her and not try to fake her out. That usually doesn't work well with horses. So it's best to be honest. I continue brushing and feeling her warmth and steadiness. I focus on breathing in rhythm with her. I breathe to calm myself, and her breathing helps me to take long, slow inhales and exhales. I think it helps both of us feel more at ease.

It's close to showtime. We still must saddle up, warm up and make our way to the arena. Jenn helps me blanket and saddle Pi. I choose the blue-weave and southwestern-patterned blanket to go with my light blue jeans. Jenn lifts the heavy western saddle onto Pi's back and tightens the cinch belt and latigo straps. To secure the bridle we place the bit gently into Pi's mouth and the headstall (which holds the bit in her mouth) over her nose and up over her ears.

Now it's time for *me* to get into the saddle. Jenn steadies Pi while Sharon and another friend get ready to lift me onto Pi's back. My way of mounting a horse is called the "jack me up" method, at least in my personal terminology. I stand up from the wheelchair as erect and stiff as possible at the side of Pi, holding firmly to the horn and cantle of my saddle. To mount a horse, I need two lifters, one on each side of me grabbing my calves. On a count of "1, 2, 3!" they lift my stiff and straight body into the air. My right leg is swung up and over the back of the saddle, and I wriggle and situate my body until I'm comfortable.

I'm on.

Ready to ride.

I guide Pi over to the practice arena alongside many other horse-and-rider pairs, noticing how stiff and tight my body feels in the early morning air. Again, I focus on my breath and the pressure of my body in the saddle. As Pi begins to walk, I allow the movement of her back end to gently raise and lower my hips and body in steady rhythm with her. I smile and relax my shoulders, remembering all the horses and people who helped me get here today.

Pi and I are ready. We've practiced the pattern. I have it in my mind and know it in my body. I am confident that Pi will be guided true with my leadership and skill.

Warm-up is over. It's 9:12 a.m. The bell rings, Pi and I enter the event arena.

It's showtime!

P.S. It was a picture-perfect performance in the Novice Division—blue ribbon.

29

Last Ride

"Heart murmur," Jenn says, as I pull my wheelchair up the dirt threshold and into the barn.

She's already busy with the grooming brush, starting to get this horse ready for me to ride. It's early Friday morning, not my usual ride time.

"What? Pi has a heart murmur. What does that mean for us?" I ask already knowing on some level what the answer will be.

"The vet came out yesterday to check her over. I've been suspecting something's up because she's just not herself these days. He said not to ride her anymore. It's too dangerous for both you and her. If her heart stops, she'll just fall over without warning. It's okay—you can have a short ride her today. One last ride."

I can't see the tears I know are streaming from Jenn's eyes; she's moved to the other side of Pi. I only hear them in her soft voice.

I'm crying too, even though I've had plenty of endings with older, mature horses over the last twelve years. I ride them for years, into their geriatric stages, forming strong bonds with each one.

"Really?" I hear myself say—not pushing back against the reality of Pi's condition—instead simply bewildered that my time with Pi will be done so soon. We have been riding partners for almost six years. We competed together in my very first para-equestrian events, taking home two blue ribbons. Our riding this summer was especially good. I'm more relaxed, more confident with her. I've been working on some new moves and skills with her graceful support.

For me, Pi is a champion. She is always patient and kind with my imbalanced muscles and occasional lack of confidence. I keep coming back, trying new things, and gaining new abilities as the years pass.

We practiced every week surrounded by the same four walls of the indoor arena, with their dusty mirrors, sometimes weaving through the orange cones, arranged in a line, at a walk or trot. We did small circles and large ones too. A light touch on the reins gave way to smoother transitions and immediate stops. We advanced to the side pass and leg yield; a different way to move a horse than the usual straight ahead or around in a circle. I could feel us in sync, breathing together.

Today though, for what is our last "ride," I take the reins and we walk slowly and gently around the old familiar arena. We spend a little more time on the far side, just to be together in our own quiet way.

"Thank you Pi," I say to her. "You helped me so much these past six years. You helped me be a more confident rider. You stretched my legs out and gave me the sensation of walking again.

You lifted me up higher than any wheelchair or crutches could. And you made me laugh with your sneezes and coughs and occasional stopping to scratch an itch on your face by bending so far forward to the front of your leg I thought I might go over the top." I say all this softly while stroking her warm belly once again.

"You helped me work out the troubles of my day. The times of caring for my mom that were so overwhelming. Or when the nursing students were driving me a little crazy. You helped me come back to the present moment, to not worry about tomorrow or be mad about yesterday. Being with you every week—even if it was for just an hour—made me a better person. I got to calm down. I got to breathe and settle into the warmth of your body. I got to be scared and tentative and work through it all. I laughed out loud and now, today, I'm crying out loud." And it was true. I felt the warm moisture of tears on my cheeks.

"I know this is the best for you. A heart murmur is a serious condition, whether you're a horse or a human. Who knows how much longer you get to live? It will be a retirement of sorts. I can learn from you about the changes that come with getting older. That might be my next big lesson."

I continue talking about hopes for the future for us both. "There is another job for you, my dear. You can help me with my student nurse program. We will be partners in a new way. I know you'll be great."

And for me? I think to myself. *Am I done riding now that you're retiring?*

It's not as easy for me to just go to the next horse available. I need some time to ponder. This isn't a situation where any old horse will do. They must be able to handle my imbalanced body and my use of tappers for leg commands. My mounting routine is not like anything most horses ever encounter. We will have to learn to trust each other and not get all crazy. The horse must be one that is reliable, consistent, and able to handle a new rider. And I must learn to trust again, to bring forth everything I learned from all the horses over these years, including you, Pi.

But that is a question I won't answer today. Instead Pi and I start walking again, enjoying our last riding time together in the dusty, sunshine-filled outdoor arena. Her walk slow and steady beneath me, my body relaxed, my breathing steady and calm, my heart filled with love and warmth for this beautiful, kind horse.

A Wholehearted Life:
It Was Not About the Walking

The accident was a big wake-up call. I could have gone back to sleep after it, but I didn't. I woke up.

The chance to wake up has been an ongoing gift. I was granted a wholehearted life. I got ahold of the thread of my life and would not let go. It turns out that the injury that seemed to take away so much actually gave me more and allowed me to live a fuller, more expansive life.

It is ironic that after getting hit by that car, slamming into the hard pavement and being left half-paralyzed, I finally learned to take the first step towards creating my life.

Before the accident I was not focused on my life. I was instead just sort of floating along: bored with teaching, with adult sports leagues, and with attempting to find myself through multiple dead-end relationships. I had no understanding that I could create the life I wanted; I was in default mode. Whatever happened, happened. I was adrift, with no ideas about becoming a true adult.

The accident knocked the crap out of me—or perhaps what was holding me back: the self-doubt, the lostness, the self-conscious focus on others and not myself. After it I learned that life is not really about the walking, but about where I choose to walk *to*; that is, what I choose to do with the life I have available. And taking that first step is most important.

After the accident I saw many other people walking in the world who seemed more paralyzed than I was. In fact, that was me before the accident. Now I wanted more. The accident helped bring that into sharp focus. It slowed me down and made me pay more attention to myself and my environment than I had before. It helped me see more clearly what I wanted from life. So I went for meaningful experiences, emotional risk-taking, stretching my comfort zone… and I realized that showing my vulnerability was more courageous than not doing so.

I made several choices to create this new life.

Grow my teaching toolbox: I yearned for the day when I could get back to my gymnasium with the middle school kids. I didn't know how it would work. I would be in a wheelchair. I had to grow in my teaching skills. No more just throwing the ball out on the field and shouting, "Let's play!" I developed more specific verbal instructions, identified kids who could demonstrate skills and got creative with classroom management. I determined that the wheelchair would not be a barrier for me. It would simply be my transportation. I would roll instead of stroll.

Explore the world: The kayak became my vehicle to the edges of the wilderness. I went to the far sides of lakes, reservoirs and oceans. On rivers, the downstream current moved me faster, swifter and easier. Horses took me places I could not go myself. I learned to trust, be a leader and be gentle in voice and touch with these big creatures. My handcycles became my road warriors and I logged hundreds of miles across the bike paths and trails of Colorado.

Go deeper into myself: The dark edge of my soul would be revealed through the years. This darkness took me to the edge of self-harm and despair. This edge would open me up to the healing, the tender points of human existence. The spinal cord injury broke open a space that allowed the light to come into the dark, closed-off area of self.

Be in relationship: This injury helped me know I was not alone in the world. I could not hide or keep myself apart any longer. I had to go forward into my humanity and share that with others. Sharon met me at a point of vulnerability. As I lay in that hospital bed, I was open and alive. She saw that, got a glimpse of me, then took hold and would not let go. I tried so many times to make her leave me as I closed back up and sealed myself off. I got to know that I was connected to and not separate from the rest of the world. I would be in relationship with this woman who never wavered in her love for me. The injury slowed me down; literally, I was not moving fast any longer. My heart was stirred, and this unconditional love touched me deeply. I learned to receive and not just give all the time. Sharon made me laugh and helped me know the joy of living and loving.

Here is my wish for you, dear reader: A wholehearted life is available to you. Your life is a gift to the world; do not hold back. Take your first step into what you want. Go for it! The cool morning air and cold waters will greet you. Use my stories as guides. Let them help you see the way forward.

I was scared many times too. I know how that feels. I can assure you that the pain of staying stuck is worse than any pain felt from taking that first step.

Step just out of your comfort zone. That's where the growth is: at the edges.

Ask for help. Know you are not alone. Notice the help that is already there—maybe you just don't see it yet. Keep your eyes and heart wide open. Keep listening to that quiet inside voice. It is calling you to your life. Pay attention, and do not go back to sleep.

There is always more life to be lived.

***

What is next for me? I plan on using my experiences and lessons to help others find their way through challenging times. I will always be a teacher, a coach, and a bright light for others in dark times. Helping others navigate the unfamiliar and find their way is the greatest joy of my life.

To share my wholehearted life. This will be my gift to the world.

Acknowledgments

I am deeply grateful to all of the many people who have supported me in this journey. Some are people I knew; some are people I got to know along the way, and others were simply angels appearing when I needed them most.

All of the many students I have encountered gave me a reason to get up in the morning, and to get back out to the playing field, university classroom and hospital patient education area. They helped me see myself again as a teacher and follow that lifelong calling.

Sandra Dorr, my writing coach, and the writing group members in Grand Junction, Colorado, for encouraging me to keep writing and providing such important feedback and reflection. You all helped me be brave and stay honest with my writing.

Kamin Samuel, my coach extraordinaire, for continued tangible support and loving encouragement to get this work ready for shipping. And for the guidance to navigate the publishing journey.

Chris Nelson, my editor who took my writing quirks in stride, and whose keen attention to detail helped guide me through the writing. I am so thankful to you for respecting my voice throughout the editing process.

Everyone who enthusiastically agreed to read the first drafts and give honest feedback and direction for improvements. I so appreciate you letting me know that the book had merit and would absolutely help at least one person in the world.

My animal companions, especially my black dogs: Shadow, Molly, and Shamly, who kept me focused on what is important in life. Your cuddles and loving kept me going.

And all those horses, who helped me come back to myself and find the ground beneath me. Your strength, kindness and presence are my saving graces.

My siblings who showed up in special ways and opportune moments to help me: Peggy, Patty, Rick and Tom. I love you all.

My parents, Pauline and Artie, who loved me no matter my condition. They demonstrated strength of character and kindness through their own lifelong struggles.

Gratitude to Spirit for the quiet voice within and loving guidance throughout this lifetime.

And, my loving partner, Sharon Lucy Blackburn. You made me laugh through tough times, loved me even when I could not love myself, and always carried the equipment so we could bike, kayak, camp and ski. I love you forever.

About the Author

Terry Chase began her early life exploring the wooded areas of Long Island, New York. Her travels as a young girl to Reno, Nevada, spurred an interest in the mountains and desert plains. Terry has always been adventurous and loves the outdoors. She is passionate about teaching and has superpowers that help make hard and complicated concepts, ideas and techniques easy to understand—and she always does it with a bit of fun!

Terry brings the valuable life-experience of living with spinal cord injury for over thirty years to her work helping others with creating a vision for the future and developing the practical steps to move forward.

She is a highly educated individual with numerous degrees and certifications, most of which she attained after the her spinal cord injury, most notably her Doctorate of Nursing. Terry lives full-out and is active in all things outdoors, including kayaking, cross-country skiing, hand-cycling and—whenever possible—horseback riding. Terry, her partner, Sharon, their two dogs and a cat reside in Western Colorado, in the shadow of the Colorado National Monument.

Work with Terry

Dr. Terry Chase offers coaching, consulting, and speaking with a deep and multi-faceted background of advanced education and hands-on experience in healthcare, education, and professional development.

Taking her love of experiential learning from outdoor education to corporate and healthcare teams, her work with clients spans the organizational, educational and healthcare systems. She offers conference keynotes, experiential workshops and break-out sessions in effective leadership, communication, team skill and education practices, as well as a nursing fellowship to develop extraordinary leaders within hospitals.

As a professional coach, Dr. Chase offers clients an opportunity for new learnings and expansion on the personal and professional levels. She partners with her clients to assist them in engaging their potential and living a fulfilled life with grace and ease.

For more information about Terry, please visit:

www.drterrychase.com

Made in the USA
Las Vegas, NV
02 December 2021